This book, *Practicing P1*
and Christians in thei

MW01034176

people. The book of Proverbs has always been one of my favorite books of the Bible. I have read it and used it again and again in my own personal life, in my pastoral and counseling ministry and in my attempts to bring my children up in the discipline and instruction of the Lord. To this point, I have been helped greatly by Charles Bridge's commentary on Proverbs. Now, Richard Mayhue's book comes alongside the book by Bridges to provide valuable insights into the practicality of Proverbs and to arrange the Proverbs in a topical way that will make the book even more useful. I heartily encourage Christians to purchase the book, read it, heed it and put its truths into practice in their lives and ministries.

Dr. Wayne Mack
Professor of Biblical Counseling
The Master's College

Dr. Mayhue's book fills a long-awaited need. It makes the Proverbs accessible. This book becomes a catalog of proberbial principles and illustrations easily found. The opening chapters are a rich treatment of the nature of wisdom and the priority of fearing the Lord. The latter half of the book provides indexes by which the individual Proverbs can be accessed. This is a marvelous tool for the Bible student, as well as a rich resource for every reader.

Dr. John MacArthur, Pastor
Grace Community Church

What a delightful and refreshing spiritual treasury from the pen of Richard Mayhue! Proverbs is indeed the most practical book in the Bible, and I love it! I definitely fit the multi-audience to whom this volume is addressed: I love a good devotional book, especially when it offers a plan for discipleship that can be used in any setting; add to that counseling tips for the hurting people who cross my paths; I also love wisdom to enhance my grandparenting and illustrations for making my Bible teaching come alive, not to mention a resource for living the Christian life and affirming a biblical worldview. The volume is a must for my personal and classroom use and for yours!

Dr. Dorothy Kelley Patterson
Professor of Theology in Women's Studies
Southwestern Baptist Theological Seminary

Practicing Proverbs is one of the most practical books you will ever read! Why? Because of the manner in which author Richard Mayhue bases his thoughts and unique arrangement of materials on the Book of Proverbs – one of the most helpful books of the Bible.

I personally know that ever since Mayhue's conversion (which occurred while he was a U.S. Naval officer) he has incorporated these same principles into his daily life, and with tremendous effect. You too can experience the same great blessing in your life. I would strongly encourage everyone to read this book!

Dr. Tim LaHaye
Author, Minister, Educator

RICHARD MAYHUE

PRACTICING PROVERBS

WISE LIVING FOR FOOLISH TIMES

November 2007

Ed –

May the Lord bless
your labors on
His behalf.

CHRISTIAN FOCUS

ISBN 1-85792-777-X

© Copyright Richard Mayhue 2003

Published in 2003,
Reprinted 2004
by
Christian Focus Publications Ltd, Geanies House,
Fearn, Tain, Ross-shire, IV20 1TW, Scotland

www.christianfocus.com

Cover Design by Alister MacInnes

Printed and bound by
Cox & Wyman, Reading, Berkshire

Contents

DEDICATION

To James Patrick, the newest Mayhue, with a grandfather's prayer
that your life will be shaped by Proverbs' spiritual chisels to
resemble the One in whom are hidden all the treasures of wisdom
and knowledge (Colossians 2:3).

INTRODUCTION

American and British literature contains thousands of proverbs. They represent a potpourri of time-tested, common-sense aphorisms, many of which have their origins in other countries and date even before the actual establishment of America as a sovereign nation. I remember reading about an elementary school teacher who, wanting to convey creatively some of these national and international proverbs to her students, decided to provide the first part of the proverb and then have her young learners fill in the remainder. One little girl received, "A bird in the hand...."The teacher expected to hear, "...is worth two in the bush.", but this youngster blurted out "...is sure to go to the bathroom!" While I am certain that there is truth in both versions, I want to write about the Jewish Proverbs of Scripture with a far more serious intent than comes from this humorous incident or even from helpful proverbs of mere human origin.

I first visited Russia (then the USSR) in February 1991, and have returned several times since (now a part of the Commonwealth of Independent States [CIS]). It struck me then that here stands a prominent nation which desperately needs a completely new set of absolute ethical and moral principles, i.e. Proverbs, to guide both the government and the people as they transition through violently dramatic spiritual, economic, political, ethical, and social upheavals, caused partly by their many decades of government-imposed, national atheism.

The same need exists in my own country – the United States of America. If I had one message to give the CEOs, educators, political leaders, media pundits, and social scientists of our day, it would be the teaching of Proverbs, which majors on making one wise unto salvation in Jesus Christ (Prov 30:2–4; 2 Tim 3:14–15) and teaching the wisest way to live for God's glory.

Proverbs' clear message rings so compellingly and powerfully that one commentator of another era (Charles Bridges, *A Commentary on Proverbs*, xiv) concluded, "Doubtless, if the world were governed by the whole wisdom of this single book, it would be a new earth, wherein dwelleth righteousness." If Proverbs' wisdom has the potential to change the entire world, imagine what it could do for you and your family.

What a noble motivation to start learning about God's wisdom! With that in mind, I have prepared *Practicing Proverbs* for you who personally want to embrace and deposit God's eternal wisdom (Proverbs) in your own life or in the life of someone else for whom you spiritually care. The format has matured slowly over the years – fueled by my fascination with the sanctified practicality of Proverbs, but also by my frustration over the lack of usable discipleship/ devotional material with substance to guide one's study through this inexhaustible treasury of wisdom.

Almost all volumes on Proverbs present their material either in commentary form or in abridged, selected-topics form that lacks the maximum value of a comprehensive, unabridged, thematic presentation that enables the reader to gain closure on any given topic. Currently, to the best of my knowledge, no such book exists in print like *Practicing Proverbs*, which easily allows the reader full access to Proverbs' practical riches.

Practicing Proverbs intends to be a guide to glorifying God[1] by living wisely. Paul writes, "So, whether you eat or drink or whatever you do, do all to the glory of God" (1 Cor 10:31). Every part of a Christian's life should be dedicated to this honorable end.

Practicing Proverbs delivers the complete content of the greatest collection of divine wisdom ever written. This book's layout presents

---

1. For an expanded discussion about "glorifying God," see Richard Mayhue, *Seeking God: How to Develop an Intimate Spiritual Relationship* (Fearn, Ross-shire, Great Britain: Christian Focus, 2000), 227–233.

God's wisdom in a life-related format with 52 themes organized under six life applications. Because much of Proverbs can be understood at face value, the presentation provides no commentary, although several accompanying introductory/explanatory chapters add related historical and biblical points of interest. Additional bibliographic resources appear below which can aid the reader when undertaking expanded studies. Five indexes will assist the user to find quickly the verse(s) or section needed. The sample **Strategy for Spiritual Success Worksheet** will equip you to keep a Proverbs diary of sorts to record your spiritual progress. Every quoted Scripture comes from the English Standard Version (ESV) unless otherwise noted.

Practicing Proverbs represents the most multi-audience book I have ever written – actually nine books in one. First, it can be employed as a devotional book for family or personal use. Second, it is a discipleship book to be used in the local church, small groups, or family discipleship. Third, it provides a Bible study book that can be selected for group study on Sunday or during the week. Fourth, it supplies a biblical counseling book that will serve not only as a ready reference for the counselor, but also as a help for the counselee. Fifth, it acts as a grandparent's book, i.e. a volume from which to pass on eternal wisdom to grandchildren. Sixth, it serves as a Proverbs illustration book for pastors and Bible teachers who are looking to shed light on ethical teachings found elsewhere in the Old and New Testaments. Seventh, it functions as a reference volume for pastors, Sunday school teachers, or individuals to pull together rapidly all of the Proverbs on a particular topic. Eighth, it comes as a ready-made resource for the Christian school teacher and missionary to teach ethics, morality, and values from a biblical perspective. Ninth, it can be enlisted by a nation's, state's, or city's school system to teach a Christian perspective on living.

Let me suggest that you begin mastering God's wisdom with a basic, thirteen-month approach to *Practicing Proverbs*. First, take one month and read one chapter of Proverbs each day. This will acquaint you with the content. Second, take the next year to study each of the fifty-two themes developed in this book, according to the plan outlined in the

Devotional Index. Record your thoughts, conclusions, and intentions on the **Strategy for Spiritual Success Worksheet** (sample included at the back of this book). By the end of the year, you should begin to have a firm grip on God's wisdom. Then, keep yourself refreshed by annually reading through Proverbs, one chapter a day, in one month.

I recommend the following resources to enhance your study of Proverbs and to provide help with verses that are hard to understand.

Alden, Robert L. *Proverbs: A Commentary on an Ancient Book of Timeless Advice*. Grand Rapids, MI: Baker, 1983.

Bridges, Charles. *A Commentary on Proverbs*. Edinburgh: Banner of Truth, 1979, rpt. of 1846 ed.

Bullock, C. Hassell. *An Introduction to the Old Testament Poetic Books*. rev. ed. Chicago, IL: Moody, 1988.

Goldberg, Louis. *The Practical Wisdom of Proverbs*. Grand Rapids, MI: Kregel, 1999.

House, H. Wayne and Kenneth M. Durham. *Living Wisely in a Foolish World*. Grand Rapids, MI: Kregel, 1997.

Kidner, Derek. *The Proverbs: An Introduction and Commentary*. Downers Grove, IL: IVP, 1969.

Lane, Eric. *Proverbs*. Fearn, Ross-shire, Scotland: Christian Focus Publications, 1999.

MacArthur, John. *Successful Christian Parenting*. Nashville, TN: Word, 1998. Especially Chapter Four, "Teaching Your Children Wisdom," 69–104.

Morris, Henry M. *The Remarkable Wisdom of Solomon*. Green Forest, AR: Master Books, 2001.

Steveson, Peter A. *A Commentary on Proverbs*. Greenville, SC: BJU Press, 2001.

Wiersbe, Warren W. *Be Skillful*. Wheaton, IL: Victor, 1995.

Zuck, Roy B. ed. *Learning from the Sages: Selected Studies on the Book of Proverbs*. Grand Rapids, MI: Baker, 1995.

To help you see how *Practicing Proverbs* unfolds, here is a preview. It begins with the bittersweet autobiography of Solomon who wrote most of Proverbs. The wisest man ever to live recounts how he failed **Wisdom's Final Exam** in Ecclesiastes, even though he personally authored the textbook. Next comes an introduction to **Wisdom's Only Authorized Textbook** that answers some of the most often asked questions about Proverbs' background. Following this, **Wisdom's Beginning** points to the unique starting place for anyone who truly seeks to be wise. Then, **Wisdom's Wind** explains various features of wisdom, extending from "where to find it" all the way to "how it is acquired." **Wisdom's Way Is Best**, a repeated theme in Proverbs, completes the first five chapters.

The final six chapters of *Practicing Proverbs* do not discuss the Proverbs, but rather they contain the actual Proverbs rearranged from the biblical order into life situations catalogued by various proverbial themes. Organized into six life-applications – spiritual, personal, family, intellectual, marketplace, and societal, the 915 verses of Proverbs showcase 52 themes.

Now, the best way to begin your quest for God's wisdom starts with the author of Proverbs and his unique life. You can learn much from Solomon's failure to pass **Wisdom's Final Exam**.

Richard Mayhue
September 2003

1

WISDOM'S FINAL EXAM[2]

At 2:20am on April 15, 1912, the impossible happened – the unsinkable ship sank. The most celebrated cruise ship in history nose-dived to the bottom of the North Atlantic. She had sailed four days earlier from Southampton, England, on her maiden voyage en route to New York; no expense had been spared to make it the most extravagant cruise ever. All went according to schedule until Sunday night when the *Titanic* sailed into an ice field.

She had received four warnings of impending danger that day from ships who were in the midst of the ice, but chose to ignore all four; several did not even reach the bridge or the captain. At 11:00 pm that Sunday night, the wireless operator, John Phillips, received a direct warning call from the *California*, which was ten miles away in the midst of some very large ice.

Phillips grew tired, having sent messages all day to America. So, that night he cavalierly tapped back, "Shut up, shut up, I'm busy." Forty minutes later the beloved ship of the White Star Line collided with an ice behemoth. Within hours, the Titanic rested in her watery grave along with 1,500 passengers and crew – certainly one of the world's great human disasters.

---

2. This chapter has been adapted and expanded from Richard Mayhue, "Solomon: The Shipwrecked Saint," in *Fight the Good Fight: Learning from Winners and Losers in the Bible* (Fearn, Ross-shire, Great Britain: Christian Focus, 1999), 10–25.

Solomon's kingdom proved to be the *Titanic* among Hebrew reigns. He possessed wealth and wisdom; his kingdom enjoyed unprecedented peace, promise, and prosperity. Israel seemed unsinkable. God had warned the captain about life's navigational hazards but, with wild abandon, Solomon ordered full speed ahead. Violent collisions with four devastating icebergs resulted; the good ship Israel capsized and the hopes of God's blessing sank with her. The sinking of Israel with Solomon at the helm ranks as one of the world's great spiritual disasters.

In Ecclesiastes, Solomon recounts the horrors of collision-at-sea as God's caution to all who sail the same waters of life. So that you can grasp what Solomon is saying, I first want to summarize the background of Ecclesiastes as a framework for your thinking.

Ecclesiastes involves the despairing, but spiritually useful, autobiography written by Solomon in his twilight years. Here, he rehearses the utter uselessness of squandering God's means and wealth to accomplish one's personal ends, thus adding to earthly pleasures which do not honor or glorify God. He begins with this well-known phrase, "Vanity of vanities! All is vanity" (Eccl 1:2). He ends that way, too. "Vanity of vanities...all is vanity" (12:8). This same idea appears 36 times in between. What a tragedy in the life of Solomon! He will be remembered for being derelict in his kingly duties.

The following question begs for an answer. "How did the glorious and seemingly invincible King Solomon and his kingdom Israel come to such a disastrous end?" By application, you need to ask, "What can I learn from Solomon so that my life never reproduces a pitiful portrait like the one I see painted in Ecclesiastes?" Pay careful attention as Solomon's life sounds the alarm to be on the watch for these spiritual icebergs: 1) misdirected wisdom, 2) misused wealth, 3) multiplied women, and 4) mixed worship.

Solomon's spiritual heritage

God gave David, concerning his son Solomon, one of the greatest *promises* in the Bible. "When your days are fulfilled and you lie down with your fathers...I will establish his kingdom. He shall build a house for my name, and I will establish the throne of his kingdom forever" (2 Sam 7:12–13).

On his deathbed, David expectantly passed that charge on to his son Solomon:

> When David's time to die drew near, he commanded Solomon his son, saying, "I am about to go the way of all the earth. Be strong, and show yourself a man, and keep the charge of the Lord your God, walking in his ways and keeping his statutes, his commandments, his rules, and his testimonies, as it is written in the Law of Moses, that you may prosper in all that you do and wherever you turn, that the Lord may establish his word that he spoke concerning me, saying, 'If your sons pay close attention to their way, to walk before me in faithfulness with all their heart and with all their soul, you shall not lack a man on the throne of Israel.'" (1 Kings 2:1–4)

Later, God personally delivered that message to Solomon in a dream (1 Kings 3:14). If that were not enough, 1 Kings 8 describes Solomon dedicating the temple for the entire nation, where he prays about the very same promises that God had given to him earlier (8:22–61). Then God reappeared before Solomon to restate and reaffirm these promises. (1 Kings 9:1–9).

Not only did Solomon hold the *promises* that God had given to him, but he also possessed the *precepts* that had been delivered to the prophets before Solomon, in particular those of Moses, who wrote the first five books in the Old Testament. There, God gave Moses a record for future kings – the very precepts that should have guarded Solomon from coming near any one of the succession of four icebergs with which he finally collided.

God had clearly warned, "Don't misdirect My wisdom." The way to have a wise reign for Israel involved not only knowing the Word of God, but day-by-day being in it, reading it, and obeying it (Deut 17:18–20). Also, kings were not to seek wealth aggressively;

and the king was to set the example for the entire kingdom and walk in the ways that God had first ordained for Adam and Eve, by having a monogamous marriage. "Only he must not acquire many horses for himself or cause the people to return to Egypt in order to acquire many horses, since the Lord has said to you, 'You shall never return that way again.' And he shall not acquire many wives for himself, lest his heart turn away, nor shall he acquire for himself excessive silver and gold" (Deut 17:16–17). The Scriptures also spoke clearly that the nation and the king, setting the example, were to render uncompromising devotion to Almighty God (Deut 17:2–5).

So God instructed Israel in effect, "If you want a pure kingdom, there are four things to avoid – misdirected wisdom, misused wealth, multiplied women, and mixed worship." Solomon had received *promises*; Solomon had been given *precepts*. Some of his 3,000 *proverbs* were later published in the biblical book of Proverbs. With these, he ably warned others about the very hazards that eventually caused his ruin.

Then, how did this spiritual disaster happen? With all of these promises, precepts, and proverbs, how could Solomon have blundered so badly and misused what God had given him? How did Solomon ever end up as a shipwrecked saint? Regardless of how it all took place, be warned of this – it did happen to Solomon and it could happen to you.

Look at Ecclesiastes where Solomon recounts the horrors of his tragically sinful life. By learning from him, you will want to chart a different course, one that navigates around the dangerous icebergs that long ago sank the good ship Israel with Solomon in command.

Misdirected wisdom

Solomon teaches that the initial iceberg to avoid is misdirected wisdom. One day God appeared to Solomon in a dream (1 Kings 3:3–14) and asked, in effect, "If you could have anything you wanted, ask for it, because I'm so minded to give it to you" (v. 5).

Solomon responded, "I would like to have wisdom in order to judge between good and evil and to rule the nation of Israel in your stead, Lord" (v. 9). God said, "You have answered so well and so faithfully that not only will I give you the wisdom, but I will give you wealth and peace and prosperity and all the rest that goes with the kingdom."

God gifted wisdom to Solomon in an unprecedented way (vv. 10–13). As a result, he could discern the difference between good and evil, lead the nation, and claim to be the wisest man who ever lived at that time or who ever would live in all time. He gained an international reputation (4:29–34); people came from all around to look in wonder at the wisdom of Solomon and to see if, in fact, he lived up to his global fame.

Solomon authentically measured up to the claims that went forth from his kingdom. He was everything that God had intended him to be, and seemingly, a little bit more. But his life took a different turn than expected. What happened? Read Ecclesiastes 1:13–18.

And I applied my heart to seek and to search out by wisdom all that is done under heaven. It is an unhappy business that God has given to the children of man to be busy with. I have seen everything that is done under the sun, and behold, all is vanity and a striving after wind. What is crooked cannot be made straight, and what is lacking cannot be counted. I said in my heart, "I have acquired great wisdom, surpassing all who were over Jerusalem before me, and my heart has had great experience of wisdom and knowledge." And I applied my heart to know wisdom and to know madness and folly. I perceived that this also is but a striving after wind. For in much wisdom is much vexation, and he who increases knowledge increases sorrow.

Remember that Solomon was looking back at life from his latter years and telling what it had been like. The wisdom that God had given him eventually brought only emptiness. It didn't satisfy. It became vanity. He looked for additional wisdom, believing that God's wisdom proved insufficient. Driven by doubt, he unnecessarily tried to test God's wisdom, even though it was infallible and inexhaustible from the beginning.

Why such a strange response? Solomon basically remained unsatisfied and unwilling to minister without doubting the wisdom that God had given him by direct revelation; rather, he tested God's wisdom by human reason and empirical research. He went beyond and against divinely bestowed wisdom in order to check it out. He failed to accept God's wisdom by faith, and thereby misdirected the Lord's wisdom and violated God's intention. He set aside the wisdom of God in favor of fallen man's skewed profundity, and stretched God's perfect truth all out of shape. When that was done, he had seemingly dethroned God and deified man, much like Eve in Genesis 3. But, God had never intended for that to happen.

One commentator paraphrased the words of Solomon, "I did succeed in becoming a great man, so had access to resources that others did not have. And besides, I grew in wisdom above all that had ever been before me over the people of God; in fact, by honest mental effort I added to the natural capacities that God had given me, acquiring 'wisdom and knowledge' in abundance."

Solomon, like so many human intellectuals, struggled for an entire lifetime to scale the highest mountains of learning. Then, in the last days of his life and exhausted by the journey, he pulled himself over the final obstacles only to meet face-to-face with Almighty God, who had been there for all eternity. Solomon let loose an unforgettable cry of agony and emptiness. His best human efforts to edit the wisdom of God had proved futile. Listen to his instructive confession.

> Then I said in my heart, "What happens to the fool will happen to me also. Why then have I been so very wise?" And I said in my heart that this also is vanity. For of the wise as of the fool there is no enduring remembrance, seeing that in the days to come all will have been long forgotten. How the wise dies just like the fool! So I hated life, because what is done under the sun was grievous to me, for all is vanity and a striving after wind (Eccl 2:15–17).

What a sad commentary on such a distinguished person's life. Looking back, he undoubtedly remembered the promises; Solomon surely recalled the precepts that he previously affirmed as true in Proverbs, but failed to practice and thus misdirected the wisdom God gave him. So he wrote Ecclesiastes to say, in effect, "People, learn from me! Life is empty; it brings tears to my eyes and pain to my heart. Be warned. Don't walk where I walked. Don't live as I lived. Accept God's wisdom by faith; don't test it. Use it with an eternal perspective to know good rather than with an earthly view to know the pain and folly of evil." The only true wisdom that is satisfying, valuable, and has eternal worth comes from God alone to be deployed in human efforts that put His glory on display.

Misused wealth

The remaining three icebergs broke off from that of misdirected wisdom. The second berg is misused wealth. Someone remarked recently that the futility of riches is stated very plainly in two places – in the income tax form and in the Bible. But, no one says it better than King Solomon in Ecclesiastes 2:1–11.

First Kings gives a few insights into the riches and wealth of Solomon's life. First Kings 4:26 recounts that Solomon had amassed 40,000 horses. Peace reigned on all borders of his kingdom, which started in the east from the Euphrates, continued to the west on the Mediterranean, and extended all the way south to Egypt (5:4). In 1 Kings 7:1–8, read about the bungalow he built for himself and his wife. The construction took 13 years – twice as long as it took him to build the house of God. He stood as the richest and wisest man on the globe. People came from the four corners of the earth and added to his wealth by bringing him gifts (10:23–25). The world had never before seen a man with such a grand life experience.

First Kings 10:27 contains this interesting sentence: "And the king made silver as common in Jerusalem as stone." The parallel passage (2 Chron 1:15) notes that both silver and gold were so multiplied and so plenteous that they were just as common as the little pebbles in the stream. Not only that, but he made cedars as abundant as sycamore trees. The Lebanon cedars mentioned here would be the equivalent of the sequoia redwoods in California. Imagine sequoia redwoods in everybody's backyard! And they all belonged to Solomon.

What a tremendous kingdom. He possessed houses, vineyards, parks, fruit trees, ponds, slaves, herds, treasures, singers, and concubines. You name it, he had it. It cannot be fully imagined what Solomon's luxurious life was like, much less all that God had given to him. However, I have concluded that the most sorry life in all of the Bible, second only to Judas, is the life of Solomon. He possessed all of the delights, all of the provisions, and all of the revelation of God, yet he squandered them for his own pleasure and satisfaction rather than to accomplish God's purposes.

Ecclesiastes 2:1–11 provides the real key to understanding Solomon's heart. Let me point out a couple of phrases in the text that expose Solomon's thinking in his earlier years. Solomon sinfully said to himself, "I will test you with pleasure," instead of rightly allowing God to test him (2:1). In verse 3 he thought, in effect, "I'm going to explore all the things that are done under heaven." Do you know where his mind should have been? Not on the things of earth but on the things above – on the things of God. He should have been focused on God's pleasure, not his own. He should have been walking by faith, not by sight.

Consider Solomon's boasts, "I made myself...parks" (2:5). "I made myself pools" (2:6). He tested and experienced the pleasures of men (2:8). Then, he talks about not withholding from his heart anything sensuous, undisciplined, or reckless (2:10). Following that, he cries out and expands on what it accomplished. "Then I considered all that my hands had done and the toil I had expended in doing it, and behold, all was vanity and a striving after wind, and there was nothing to be gained under the sun" (2:11). It certainly accomplished nothing of spiritual value.

Solomon misused his God–given wealth to satisfy himself rather than asking the question, "How can I invest in God's kingdom for

God's glory and for the good of God's people?" And, he found the end result to be completely unsatisfactory, even empty.

Now, there is nothing wrong with wealth. However, when you think you obtained it by yourself, and you begin to spend it selfishly with utter disregard for the plans of the one who provided it, you are on the path of futility. That proved to be the downfall of Solomon as he increasingly became self-centered, self-satisfied, and self-consumed.

Multiplied women

Now, his encounter with the third iceberg spelled the beginning of the end for Solomon, for his sons, and for the kingdom of Israel. He recklessly crashed into the berg of multiple women.

> And I find something more bitter than death: the woman whose heart is snares and nets, and whose hands are fetters. He who pleases God escapes her, but the sinner is taken by her. Behold, this is what I found, says the Preacher, while adding one thing to another to find the scheme of things – which my soul has sought repeatedly, but I have not found. One man among a thousand I found, but a woman among all these I have not found. See, this alone I found, that God made man upright, but they have sought out many schemes. (Eccl 7:26–29)

Solomon did begin the right way. Learn about his first courtship and marriage to a young Jewish girl in The Song of Solomon. So, where did Solomon come up with these words of woe? He followed a long line of men preceding him who had multiple women. You can read elsewhere in Scripture about Lamech, Abraham, Esau, Jacob, Moses, Gideon, Elkanah, Saul, and Solomon's father, David. Embracing the worldly philosophy of "more is better" contributed to his downfall.

Solomon married a woman whose name was Naamah (2 Chron 12:13), an Ammonite princess. She gave birth to Rehoboam, who ultimately became king of the Southern Kingdom when God violently ripped the united kingdom in two. Later, Solomon formed a political alliance with Pharaoh of Egypt, who ruled to the south. Conforming to that day's culture, he married one of Pharaoh's daughters to seal the covenant treaty (1 Kings 3:1). When all of Solomon's efforts to secure peace and to satisfy his sensual lust had come to an end, he had accumulated no less than 700 wives and 300 concubines (1 Kings 11:3). That proved to be 999 too many women.

This sketches the background to Ecclesiastes 7. Only one of the 1,000 women with whom he associated himself had proven to be righteous – the Shulammite maiden mentioned in The Song of Solomon. Later, he habitually sought wives from outside of the nation, and foolishly married for reasons other than those which God had given in Genesis. "Therefore a man shall leave his father and his mother and hold fast to his wife, and they shall become one flesh" (Gen 2:24).

In disobedience to God's Word, he had matrimonially joined himself to these foreign women who were outside of the faith (Ex 34:12–16; Deut 7:1–3; Josh 23:12–13). Solomon supplies a great lesson for those who entertain ideas of "evangelistic" dating. "I'll just date this good-looking guy (or girl) who doesn't know Christ, and sooner or later he (she) will come to the Savior." Let Solomon's sin serve as a stern warning: don't date outside the faith, much less marry outside the faith.

The most indicting statement concerning Solomon's marital escapades came from the pen of Nehemiah, 500 years after Solomon's reign. "Did not Solomon king of Israel sin on account of such women? Among the many nations there was no king like him, and he was beloved by his God, and God made him king over all Israel. Nevertheless, foreign women made even him to sin" (Neh 13:26).

Some time ago I was reading about William Jennings Bryan (1860–1925), a famous American lawyer and politician, and his dating years. He met a lovely young lady, fell in love with her, and decided the right thing to do was to go and ask her father for her hand in marriage. Knowing that the father had strong religious beliefs, he thought it might be helpful to quote some Scripture. So, he chose Solomon in Proverbs 18:22: "He who finds a wife finds a good thing." The father responded from Paul's writings, "So then he who marries his betrothed does well, and he who refrains from marriage will do even better" (1 Cor 7:38).

If Bryan was alive today and asked my advice on what to say next, I would direct him to Ecclesiastes 9:9 where Solomon, sobered in his waning years, reaffirms the sanctity of a one-woman relationship in marriage. "Enjoy life with the wife whom you love, all the days of your vain life that he has given you under the sun, because that is your portion in life and in your toil at which you toil under the sun." Solomon concludes, in effect, "Guys, the greatest reward you're ever going to get out of life is the wife that God gives you."

Mixed worship

One final iceberg inflicted fatal damage on Solomon. Through his multiplied wives, Solomon made himself vulnerable to the crashing waves of God's coming wrath as he hit the berg of mixed worship. Everybody knows the name of Solomon, which means peace or peaceful; but none knew him as did God. God gave Solomon a special name (2 Sam 12:25); *Jedidiah* means "beloved of the Lord." What an endearing name – almost as intimate as "this is My beloved Son," which God used of the Lord Jesus Christ. And yet this very one, beloved of the Lord, prostituted his covenant relationship with God. Following the lead of his wives, he went after strange gods. Solomon explained this in Ecclesiastes 5:1–7.

> Guard your steps when you go the house of God. To draw near to listen is better than to offer the sacrifice of fools, for they do not know that they are doing evil. Be not rash with your mouth, nor let your heart be hasty to utter a word before God, for God is in heaven and you are on earth. Therefore

let your words be few. For a dream comes with much business, and a fool's voice with many words. When you vow a vow to God, do not delay paying it, for he has no pleasure in fools. Pay what you vow. It is better that you should not vow than that you should vow and not pay. Let not your mouth lead you into sin, and do not say before the messenger that it was a mistake. Why should God be angry at your voice and destroy the work of your hands? For when dreams increase and words grow many, there is vanity; but God is the one you must fear.

Let me fill in some background here. First Kings 11:4–8 sadly reports that Solomon's multiplied wives turned his heart away from Almighty God and directed it to worship dead idols. He constructed temples in Jerusalem to worship the Astoreth, Milcom, Chemosh, and Molech – a whole multitude of foreign deities. The builder of God's temple actually constructed houses of worship for most known idols in his day. Jerusalem turned from a place that was singularly devoted to worshiping Jehovah God into one that was spiritually polluted beyond imagination. Religious pluralism plagued the nation.

In so doing, Solomon violated the first three of God's ten commandments. He had other gods (Ex 20:3). He made graven images (Ex 20:4). On top of worshiping other gods, Solomon made vows to them and thus took the name of the Lord in vain (Ex 20:7).

Understandably, God's patience eventually came to an end; his mercy ceased.

Therefore the Lord said to Solomon, "Since this has been your practice and you have not kept my covenant and my statutes that I have commanded you, I will surely tear the kingdom from you and will give it to your servant. Yet for the sake of David your father I will not do it in your days, but I will tear it out of the hand of your son. However, I will not tear away all the kingdom, but I will give one tribe to your son, for the sake of David my servant and for the sake of Jerusalem that I have chosen" (1 Kings 11:11–13).

What a sad day for Solomon! This man's wisdom had been so great that Jesus compared himself to Solomon in Matthew 12:42, "Something greater than Solomon is here." Since Solomon's wealth had so exceeded that of others, he was the only fair comparison in Matthew 6:29 when Jesus extolled the riches of God's created world. This great man lost his kingdom, his all.

As a result, Solomon warned in Ecclesiastes 5, "Learn from my mistakes; I will tell you the vanity of the sacrifice of fools. Make sure your worship is right and pure. Let me tell you about the emptiness of multiplied words and dreams. Walk into the presence of God and know that he, and he alone, is holy."

Take special note of his words in Ecclesiastes 5:7: "For when dreams increase and words grow many, there is vanity; but God is the one you must fear." Deuteronomy 17:19 gives that instruction for kings, including Solomon, to fear God by obeying His commandments. This last idea proves critically important: "God is the one you must fear."

The theme of "fearing God" (seven times) appears as the one positive thread woven throughout Ecclesiastes: "I perceived that whatever God does endures forever; nothing can be added to it, nor anything taken from it. God has done it, so that people fear before him" (3:14). "It is good that you should take hold of this, and from that withhold not your hand, for the one who fears God shall come out from both of them" (7:18). "Though a sinner does evil a hundred times and prolongs his life, yet I know that it will be well with those who fear God, because they fear before him" (8:12; also see 5:7; 8:13).

Solomon concluded his autobiography at 12:13–14. In his last years, he recognized how grievously sinful he had been, and repented of his iniquity. Solomon then warned future generations about the miserable failures of his life, an alert that has been preserved for almost 3,000 years. "The end of the matter; all has been heard. Fear God and keep his commandments, for this is the whole duty of man. For God will bring every deed into judgment, with every secret thing, whether good or evil."

Think about eternity

Let me ask you one final question: how are you doing in the areas of wisdom, wealth, women (or men), and worship? As a point of reference, review what God will one day judge as good, if they are the pattern or habit of your life: 1) a faith response to God's revelation that needs no human reason or empirical research for verification or amplification; 2) a pilgrim's perspective on wealth, which recognizes that it comes from God to spend for God's glory by investing it in the Lord's work instead of the passing pleasures of life; 3) a one-woman (or one-man) mentality, which preserves the purity of marriage and the dignity of women (or men); and 4) an uncompromising devotion to God and God alone – nothing added to dilute, nothing taken away to diminish. These four qualities encompass the defining proofs of fearing God. If these features accurately portray your life, it will be judged as good. If not, you need to repent of your sin like Solomon and take a new course in life, the wise way of Proverbs.

I close with an instructive story about a man who also faced the same spiritual ice fields that confronted Solomon. As this aspiring New York lawyer sat early one morning in the law office, God's quiet voice began to ask him, "What are you going to do when you finish your course?" He thought a minute and responded, "Well, I think I'll put out a shingle and practice law." God responded, "Then what?" He said, "I'll get rich." "Then what?" "Oh, I think I'll retire." "Then what?" "I'll probably die." "Then what?" "Judgment!"

As the word *judgment* sounded from his lips, he abruptly recognized that all he did in life would one day be brought before the bar of God, and then judgment would be rendered either for or against him. Being so moved by that experience, he immediately submitted his life, even his entire being, to Jesus Christ.

Follow this man's lead, and you will sail clear of the icebergs that sank Israel. You will avoid being ripped and scarred like Solomon, the shipwrecked saint, because you have chosen to fear God and obey His commandments. "The fear of the Lord is the beginning of wisdom, and the knowledge of the Holy One is insight" (Prov 9:10). Wisdom's final exam will be graded by how well you live in accord with God's Word, especially in regard to wisdom, wealth, women, and worship.

I often ask my students at the end of the semester, "Now that you have taken the course, has the course taken you?" Although Solomon wrote the textbook on living wisely (Proverbs), God's curriculum on wise living had not fully captured his heart and mind until the very end of his life as he testified in Ecclesiastes. Solomon's spiritual failures, however, resulted not because he lacked knowledge, but because he fell short in the discipline of translating "knowing" into "being" and "doing." However, the author's sinful unwillingness to heed his own words does not diminish the value of Proverbs in the least, since Scripture was inspired by God and made profitable for all things spiritual (2 Tim 3:16–17). Therefore, your next appropriate step involves taking an in-depth look at Proverbs itself **– Wisdom's Only Authorized Textbook**.

2

WISDOM'S ONLY AUTHORIZED TEXTBOOK

The Bible mentions Egyptian wisdom (1 Kings 4:30), wisdom of the east (1 Kings 4:30), wisdom of Edom (Jer 49:7), and the wisdom of Babylon (Jer 50:35), among others. One of the most ancient methods to teach this wisdom, dating back at least to 3000 BC in Egypt, involves the use of proverbs. These ancient literary vehicles, usually thought of as short, pithy sayings, vividly communicate general truths in a memorable way. You would easily recognize this method of teaching from more recent proverbs such as "A rolling stone gathers no moss" or "To be penny wise is to be pound foolish." This way of passing on valuable information has proven to be an effective technique for millennia. However, nothing guarantees that these kinds of proverbs have God's certified approval.

What is a proverb and where are they in Scripture?

Solomon, son of David and king of Israel (Prov 1:1), turned proverbs into an art form as a teaching method. He masterfully penned 3,000 proverbs (1 Kings 4:32), many of which have been preserved until now in the Bible book known as Proverbs. Since these words of wisdom appear in Scripture, originally coming from the mind of

God, they uniquely comprise the only set of proverbs written in human history that the Lord guarantees to be wholly true and trustworthy. While proverbs of human origin might have borne the test of time, only biblical proverbs possess the eternal authority of God.

The Hebrew word *mâshâl* translated "proverbs" carries a broader idea than normally associated with "a proverb." It basically means "to be like," i.e. a statement that intends to reveal the actual nature of a profound truth by comparing it with common, picturesque, tangible images in life. The proverb can also take longer-than-usual forms like an ode/song (see 1:7–9:18) or a poem (see 31:10–31).

They frequently express their ideas variously in two lines (11:17), four lines (24:3–4), six lines (23:19–21), or eight lines (23:22–25). Five distinct forms of parallelism are used by Solomon: 1) identical/similar (16:18); 2) opposite (11:17); 3) expansive (10:18); 4) comparative (25:25); and 5) formal, i.e. the second line completes the idea of the first line (16:7).

Proverbs also appear outside of Proverbs. For example, look at 1 Samuel 10:11–12 or 24:13 in the Old Testament historical books or Ezekiel 12:22–23, 16:44, and 18:1–2 in the Old Testament prophetic books. Additionally, the New Testament has proverbs of its own (see Matt 9:12, 17; John 4:35, 37; 1 Cor 6:13; 14:8; 15:33). And as you probably anticipated, the New Testament frequently quotes or alludes to the Old Testament book of Proverbs, at least 38 times. For a listing, turn to Appendix One – "Proverbs in the NT" (e.g. Prov 3:11–12 (Heb 12:5–6) and Prov 27:1 (James 4:13). The most frequently used (eight times) proverb in the New Testament is 24:12 (Matt 16:27; Luke 16:15; Rom 2:6; 2 Tim 4:14; 1 Peter 1:17; Rev 2:23; 20:12–13; 22:12).

> If you say, "Behold, we did not know this," does not he who weighs the heart perceive it? Does not he who keeps watch over your soul know it, and will he not repay man according to his work? (Prov 24:12)

Beyond Proverbs, several other styles of wisdom literature appear in the Old Testament. The discourses between Job and his companions, selected Psalms (e.g. 1, 19, 32, 34, 49, 73, 78, 112, 119, 127–128, 133), the prosaic autobiography of Solomon in Ecclesiastes, and the colorfully poetic account of Solomon's first love in The Song of Solomon are all considered to be among the Old Testament wisdom books.

Who wrote Proverbs and when?

Proverbs indisputably testifies three times to Solomon's (King of Israel, ca. 970–930 BC) primary authorship (1:1; 10:1; 25:1), although he is not the only contributor nor the final editor. Other apparent writers include anonymous sages (22:17–24:34), as well as Agur (30:1–33) and Lemuel (31:1–31) whose identities also remain uncertain. Proverbs 25:1–29:27, attributed to Solomon's own composition, were over 200 years later collected and collated by wise men during Hezekiah's reign (ca. 715–686 BC).

You should not be surprised that Solomon figured so prominently in the collecting and writing of Proverbs. After all, Solomon qualified to be the wisest man of his day (1 Kings 3:28; 5:7; 10:23; 11:41), and even in all of time (1 Kings 3:12). He also wrote Psalms 72 and 127, The Song of Solomon, and Ecclesiastes.

And God gave Solomon wisdom and understanding beyond measure, and breadth of mind like the sand on the seashore, so that Solomon's wisdom surpassed the wisdom of all the people of the east and all the wisdom of Egypt. For he was wiser than all other men, wiser than Ethan the Ezrahite, and Heman, Calcol, and Darda, the sons of Mahol, and his fame was in all the surrounding nations. He also spoke 3,000 proverbs, and his songs were 1,005. He spoke of trees, from the cedar that is in Lebanon to the hyssop that grows out of the wall. He spoke also of beasts, and of birds, and of reptiles, and of fish. And people of all nations came to hear the wisdom of Solomon, and from all the kings of the earth, who had heard of his wisdom. (1 Kings 4:29–34)

What is the theme of Proverbs?

Proverbs 1:7 and 9:10 establish Proverbs' prominent theme:

The fear of the Lord is the beginning of knowledge; fools despise wisdom and instruction.

The fear of the Lord is the beginning of wisdom, and the knowledge of the Holy One is insight.

Taken together, they point in this direction – "The fear of the Lord leads to divine wisdom for righteous living." While Proverbs definitely proves to be a book about practical righteousness, it stands also as a book that assumes profound theology, especially the idea – "fear of the Lord."

The phrase "fear of the Lord" appears nineteen times in Proverbs (1:7, 29; 2:5; 3:7; 8:13; 9:10; 10:27; 14:2, 26–27; 15:16, 33; 16:6; 19:23; 22:4; 23:17; 24:21; 28:14; 31:30). With "fear of the Lord" being such a dominant idea in Proverbs, I have devoted all of Chapter 3, "Wisdom's Beginning," to explaining what it means and why it should be considered important (see also Job 28:28; Ps 111:10; Eccl 12:13–14).

The "fear of the Lord" leads to true knowledge, which in turn is translated into authentic wisdom. About knowledge and wisdom Charles Haddon Spurgeon (1834–1892) wrote,

Wisdom is the right use of knowledge. To know is not to be wise. Many men know a great deal, and are all the greater fools for it. There is no fool so great a fool as a knowing fool. But to know how to use knowledge is to have wisdom.

Books of wisdom grapple with life's most difficult issues in order to see them from the perspective of wisdom, not foolishness. Proverbs remains the one book in all human history that reveals God's wise perspective on such a wide range of life issues. Wisdom, mentioned over 115 times in Proverbs alone, carries the basic idea of being skillful in living disciplines and patterns. Used in its most literal sense, wisdom describes the artisans who skillfully made Aaron's garments (Ex 28:3) and Solomon's temple (1 Chron 22:15).

So, Proverbs teaches all about a right relationship with God (fearing the Lord) that leads to true knowledge and divine wisdom for righteous living, even practical godliness. Proverbs instructs about skillfully manifesting God's character and will in one's everyday life, making godly decisions, and being so oriented to God that one's life choices always please Him.

What is the purpose of Proverbs?

Proverbs answers the universal question, "How should I live my life?" It does not focus so much on how an individual can be successful and self-fulfilled as it does on how a person can live so as to please God. It is a book about morality, duty, ethics, values, virtues, and principles that communicate and enable one to live a life in accord with God's will. Proverbs enshrines and champions the cardinal virtues of God's righteousness in a distilled and crystallized form.

The proverbs of Scripture deserve to be called "the Proverbs of proverbs" because these are the only proverbs of divine origin. They are not proverbs of human creation alone. For the most part, they are brief and concise, pithy and memorable. They contain common-sense truisms that are stamped with divine approval. They prick the conscience, penetrate the soul, and probe the deepest recesses of the heart. By design Proverbs, being a proactive book, promotes personal holiness at the most practical levels of living.

Proverbs, written primarily by Solomon, declares and promotes the truths of God's wisdom. Ecclesiastes recalls Solomon's embarrassing testimony about the consequences when one abandons God's wisdom and starts living foolishly to satisfy personal lust for earthly pleasure. In his latter days, Solomon wrote Ecclesiastes to warn others that all he did and achieved, apart from God's wisdom, produced emptiness, vanity, futility, and foolishness. Proverbs, on the other hand, teaches how to live a wise life that will be pleasing to God and spiritually satisfying to oneself. God's wisdom in Proverbs stands in stark contrast to human folly, especially that of Solomon in Ecclesiastes.

Nothing in this life compares to Proverbs' wisdom as the richest of acquisitions. God's wisdom far exceeds even silver and gold in value for enjoying a blessed life. The greatest yield, now and in eternity, can be obtained freely from Proverbs. This "mother lode" of wisdom can be mined for a lifetime without exhausting the Scriptural source.

Proverbs provides the kind of teaching material that enables a family to carry out the instructions of Deuteronomy 6:1–9:

> Now this is the commandment, the statutes and the rules that the Lord your God commanded me to teach you, that you may do them in the land to which you are going over, to possess it, that you may fear the Lord your God, you and your son and your son's son, by keeping all his statues and his commandments, which I command you, all the days of your life, and that your days may be long. Hear therefore, O Israel, and be careful to do them, that it may go well with you, and that you may multiply greatly, as the Lord, the God of your fathers, has promised you, in a land flowing with milk and honey. Hear, O Israel: The Lord our God, the Lord is one. You shall love the Lord your God with all your heart and with all your soul and with all your might. And these words that I command you today shall be on your heart. You shall teach them diligently to your children, and shall talk of them when you sit in your house, and when you walk by the way, and when you lie down, and when you rise. You shall bind them as a sign on your hand, and they shall be as frontlets between your eyes. You shall write them on the doorposts of your house and on your gates.

The teachings in Proverbs touch on six primary areas of life. First, they address one's personal relationship with God in providing *spiritual wisdom.* Second, Proverbs deals with oneself in accumulating *personal wisdom.* Third, *family wisdom* informs the relationship of husband and wife in marriage, plus parents and children in the home. Fourth, Proverbs supplies learning principles that comprise *intellectual wisdom.* Fifth, *Marketplace wisdom* teaches one how to act wisely on the job. Sixth, Proverbs directs one's activities in the community to be characterized by *societal wisdom.*

With Christ being the repository of all wisdom (Col 2:3) and the wisdom of God (1 Cor 1:24, 30), then the wisdom of Proverbs reflects the mind of Christ (1 Cor 2:16) and rehearses the wisdom by which Jesus lived on earth (Luke 2:52). Through Proverbs "the mind of Christ" can be yours (Phil 2:5). Ultimately, Proverbs provides a primer on wise living that serves as an infallible instruction manual for one godly generation to teach their children and grandchildren how they should live and thus perpetuate divine wisdom through multiple generations.

> To know wisdom and instruction, to understand words of insight, to receive instruction in wise dealing, in righteousness, justice, and equity; to give prudence to the simple, knowledge and discretion to the youth – Let the wise hear and increase in learning, and the one who understands obtain guidance, to understand a proverb and a saying, the words of the wise and their riddles. (Prov 1:2–6)

To whom was Proverbs written?

Proverbs begins with God in heaven (1:1–6) and ends on earth in the home (31:10–31). Unquestionably, Proverbs should be recognized as a heaven-sent book designed to be a discipleship manual for the heavenly Father to instruct his spiritual children on earth. And, in a more intimate sense, Proverbs also comprises a family manual for parents to instruct their own children in godly conduct. No portion of human relationships or earthly endeavors has been neglected or omitted. Proverbs contains all that a person needs to know, understand, and wisely live out in order to be pleasing to God and to others.

General audiences

Proverbs first addresses a general audience of individuals, regardless of gender, marital state, financial status, or station in life (Prov 1:4–5). Solomon divides his reading audience into three kinds of people based on their level of life maturity. First, "the simple" who do not know enough or are unwilling to act in accord with their knowledge to live prudently and to purposely avoid the dangers of life (1:4a). Second, "the youth" who need knowledge and discretion (1:4b). Third, "the wise" who know and understand, but continue to grow under wise guidance (1:5).

By way of application, there appear to be three entirely different audiences in mind here. The first group would be viewed in regard to the normal human maturation process, which includes: 1) children (the simple); 2) teenagers (youth); and 3) adults (the wise).

The second application refers to normal spiritual maturation after one's salvation (without regard for physical age). Perhaps the Apostle John obtained his three-fold delineation of spiritual maturity from Solomon's Proverbs (1 John 2:12–14). Spiritually speaking, these would be 1) little children (the simple); 2) young men (youth); and 3) fathers (the wise).

A third approach describes the general immaturity/maturity levels of people who have physically reached adulthood. There are foolish, childlike adults who behave with radical immaturity (the simple). Other adults act without discretion in an adolescent manner that could be characterized as immature for their age (youth). Then there are prudent, mature adults (the wise) who act their age. So, no matter who you are or where you are in the maturation process, Proverbs can be both a learning and a teaching tool for you.

Particular audiences

In its immediate historical context, Proverbs seems to imply that Solomon looked back to what he had learned from his father David (Prov 1:1) and mother Bathsheba (2 Sam 12:24–25). Then he anticipated what he would teach his son Rehoboam (1 Kings 11:43;

1 Chron 3:10) and other children (cf. 1 Kings 4:11, 15 which names only two daughters). Undoubtedly, with 700 wives (1 Kings 11:3), Solomon fathered far more children than are named in the Bible.

> Hear, O sons, a father's instruction, and be attentive, that you may gain insight, for I give you good precepts; do not forsake my teaching. When I was a son with my father, tender, the only one in the sight of my mother, he taught me and said to me, "Let your heart hold fast my words; keep my commandments, and live. (Prov 4:1–4)

Now, looking ahead in time, Proverbs must be applied in its ultimate sense of providing wisdom for a father (and a mother) to teach his son (and his daughter) in every succeeding generation, since the wisdom of God is eternal and unchanging. Proverbs' timeless principles are supra-cultural, supra-generational, and supra-historical.

Explicitly but not exclusively, Proverbs contains wisdom for fathers to teach their sons. "Father," mentioned at least 26 times in Proverbs, does not preclude the importance of one's "mother," mentioned fourteen times in the book. It is significant that "father and mother" are mentioned together on thirteen occasions (1:8; 4:3; 6:20; 10:1; 15:20; 17:25; 19:26; 20:20; 23:22, 25; 28:24; 30:11, 17). Not only did God intend for the father to teach his sons wisdom (1:8, 10, 15; 2:1; 3:1, 11, 21; 4:10, 20; 5:1, 20; 6:1, 3, 20; 7:1) but so too the mother (1:8; 6:20; 31:1, 28).

You might ask, "What about teaching daughters? Where do they fit in?" While not a dominant or explicit theme, it certainly is implied strongly that the lady of Proverbs 31:10–31 had been taught wisdom by her parents and that she and her husband (31:11–12, 23) were passing this wisdom along to their children by example and instruction. As a remarkably wise woman (cf. 31:30), she modeled for her sons the kind of spiritual woman whom they should marry and for her daughters the kind of godly woman that they should grow up to be. Make no mistake about it – Dad and Mom are a discipleship team in raising their children. Why else would both the

Old Testament (Ex 20:12 – 5th commandment) and the New
Testament (Eph 6:1–4) command children to honor and obey both
father and mother?

How is Proverbs organized?

After scholars divided Proverbs into chapter (ca. AD 1244) and verse
(ca. AD1528), the book contained 31 chapters and 915 verses. But
when originally written, it assumed its literary form by authorship
and/or date of writing/editing. The first edition of Proverbs most
likely included 1:1–24:34 in Solomon's time (ca. 970–930 BC). The
later edition added 25:1–31:31 in Hezekiah's day (ca. 715–686 BC).

The title of Proverbs might well be taken from Proverbs 1:1,
"The proverbs of Solomon, son of David, king of Israel." The subtitle
could be Proverbs 1:2–6.

> To know wisdom and instruction, to understand words of
> insight, to receive instruction in wise dealing, in righteousness,
> justice, and equity; to give prudence to the simple, knowledge
> and discretion to the youth – Let the wise hear and increase
> in learning, and the one who understands obtain guidance,
> to understand a proverb and a saying, the words of the wise
> and their riddles.

Proverbs could also be divided into two major sections by virtue
of its literary character. Part one (1:8–9:18), characterized by an
extended discourse, serves almost like a prologue. Then, part two
encompasses 10:1–31:31 which contains shorter sections.

However, the most complete and commonly recognized outline
designates major sections by authorship.

I.   Solomon's introduction to Proverbs   1:1–7
II. Solomon's proverbial teaching to his sons   1:8 – 9:18
III. Solomon's proverbs   10:1 – 22:16
IV. Words of the wise (men)   22:17 – 24:22
V.   Additional words of the wise (men)   24:23–34

How should Proverbs be interpreted?[3]

•   Tip 1 – Realize that no proverb or section in Proverbs intends to be an exhaustive, unabridged, final treatment of the subject at hand.

•   Tip 2 – Proverbs must be understood in terms of context which includes: 1) the language as used elsewhere in Scripture; 2) the particular section of Proverbs in which the text occurs; 3) the book of Proverbs; 4) the writings of Solomon; 5) the wisdom sections of the Old Testament; 6) the complete Old Testament; and 7) the entire Bible.

•   Tip 3 – Proverbs demands to be interpreted in the cultural and historical settings of the time in which it was written.

•   Tip 4 – Proverbs should not be taken as absolute, unconditional, guaranteed promises but rather, by definition, as generalizations that can have exceptions.

•   Tip 5 – Poetic features and figures of speech need to be taken appropriately into account when interpreting Proverbs, so that you do not interpret the text too literally.

•   Tip 6 – Be careful not to use Proverbs with the personal motive of selfish gain but rather for achieving spiritual maturity and wisdom in order to glorify God.

•   Tip 7 – If a proverb is unclear, read it in other good Bible translations (e.g. NASB or NKJV) and consult several trusted commentaries on Proverbs.

•   Tip 8 – Interpret the proverb first to determine the original intent of the author and then develop personal applications and timeless principles in light of the interpretation.

---

3. See Richard Mayhue, *How to Interpret the Bible for Yourself* (Fearn, Ross-shire, Great Britain: Christian Focus, 1999) for instructions on how to carefully study and discerningly interpret the Bible.

• Tip 9 – Proverbs is not designed for large doses of reading at one sitting, and will be most profitably studied in small portions to allow time for contemplation and reflection.

• Tip 10 – Treat Proverbs as a divine imperative for your life, not merely another optional idea coming from the secular world of wisdom.

Now, with your key questions about Proverbs answered, you are probably asking, "Where does wisdom begin and how can I obtain it?" For the answer, read on to learn about **Wisdom's Beginning**.

3

WISDOM'S BEGINNING

What do Athena (Greek), Minerva (Roman), Maat (Egyptian), Cerridwen (Celtic), Saraswati (Hindu), and Sophia (Mediterranean) have in common? They each represent their respective national, regional, or religious goddess of wisdom. The mythical stories of where wisdom came from prove bizarre at best, but none so much so as Athena, the daughter of Zeus who was the chief Olympian god in the Greek pantheon.

The legend goes that Zeus heard a prophecy that the next child his wife Metis bore after she gave birth to Athena would become the lord of heaven. So, to prevent this from happening, he swallowed Metis while she was still pregnant with Athena. When the time came for Athena to be born, Zeus had a great headache. The smith god, Hephaistos, opened Zeus' head with an axe, and Athena stepped out as the Greek goddess of wisdom. She stood as the patroness of ancient Athens which built the Parthenon on the Athenian acropolis in her honor. The owl represented her sacred bird, thus the age-old idea of "being wise as an owl." However fascinating or interesting this glimpse at ancient mythology might be, one would have to be the "fool of fools" to believe such nonsense. It certainly came from the figment of an idolatrous imagination, and has no connection whatsoever with reality.

Where did wisdom really come from, and in whom does it actually reside? Proverbs 8:22–31 personifies wisdom as a beautiful and graceful lady who poetically represents the reality of divine wisdom that is eternal and comes from God. Jesus Christ actually embodied this wisdom (Col 2:3). Paul's doxology to complete Romans says it best – "to the only wise God be glory forevermore through Jesus Christ! Amen" (16:27). God defines and supplies all true wisdom.

What is Biblical wisdom?

Wisdom comprises a dominant theme in the Old Testament (over 325 mentions in various forms). Why? Because "wisdom," like a microscope, magnifies and focuses life using the optics of Scripture in order for one to believe (embracing the truth of God) and behave (walking in the holiness of God) so as to glorify and please God, both in this life and eternity. Wisdom comes to us through God's special revelation in the Bible.

Wisdom reflects the intent and discipline to make godly choices in a world filled with sinful distractions and detours. Wisdom represents the culmination of knowing and understanding carried to its practical and ultimate end. Wisdom involves *knowing* the facts of divine revelation in Scripture, as well as *understanding* them in the sense of comprehending God's intention that they lead to a life of redemption and practical sanctification. *Wisdom* then engages the human intellect and will to translate this knowledge and understanding into a pattern of godly experience as the habit of one's life.

The Old Testament uses the concept of "wisdom" to describe several different life situations, all of which have the underlying idea of being skillful. First, there is the wise skill of an artisan in crafting something useful and/or beautiful from raw material (Ex 35:10; 1 Kings 7:14; Jer 10:9). Second, wisdom conveys the idea of being intellectually astute or skillful in observing and explaining how the natural world works. Solomon represented one such wise man (see 1 Kings 4:29–34, esp. v. 33; cf. Prov 6:6–8) as did Agur (Prov 30:15–33). Third, wisdom can also mean to apply knowledge skillfully in a common-sense way. This kind of wisdom allows one to travel through life with a minimum of obstacles and road hazards, but without any necessary regard for a personal relationship with God.

The fourth level of wisdom adds the unique dimension called the "fear of the Lord" (Prov 1:7; 9:10; 15:33). This wisdom proves not only utilitarian but also spiritual and eternal. This Scriptural wisdom can only be taught by God's Spirit to true believers who seek it (Pss 49:3; 51:6; Prov 1:1–7; 15:31–33; 22:17–21). This kind of wisdom skillfully orders a person's life in accord with the disciplined application of God's Word to accomplish God's will for God's glory. It puts God's character on extraordinary display in the ordinary course of life. It allows wisdom's practitioners to skillfully relate to people and carry out one's life responsibilities. Theoretical wisdom this is not, but rather wisdom which measures as high, as long, as deep, as wide, and as broad as the practicalities of daily living.

The ultimate expression of this divine kind of wisdom would be God's will being done on earth as it is in heaven (cf. Matt 6:10). This wisdom creates a unique quality of "kingdom culture" in a world that is fixated on human multiculturalism. Proverbs, therefore, could be described as a book not so much about theological instruction, but rather theological practice. Sanctified "uncommon" sense characterizes Proverbs. Thus, the wisest person alive knows, understands, and lives out the most about Scripture and God.

So, how does one appropriate this kind of wisdom dispensed from Proverbs? This next section answers the all-important question just raised and might be the most important portion of this chapter, perhaps even, of the entire volume. The "fear of the Lord" must be the first step taken toward God's wisdom.

What is wisdom's first step?

The "fear of the Lord" (FOL) is inseparably linked with "wisdom" in the Old Testament. FOL is the "cause" and wisdom is the "effect." Note the obvious connection in these central texts:

- Job 28:28 – FOL "is wisdom"
- Ps 111:10 – FOL "is the beginning of wisdom"

· Prov 9:10 – FOL "is the beginning of wisdom"
· Prov 15:33 – FOL "is instruction in wisdom"

FOL does not appear exclusively in Old Testament wisdom literature. It can also be seen as early as Abraham (Gen 20:11; 22:12). FOL appears at least forty-five times in the Psalms.[4] Solomon wrote about the fear of the Lord nineteen times in Proverbs, more than any other single biblical author, except David who also mentioned FOL nineteen times in the Psalms. When he penned his last words in Scripture (Eccl 12:13–14), the wisest man ever to live summarized all of life like this,

> The end of the matter, all has been heard. Fear God and keep his commandments, for this is the whole duty of man. For God will bring every deed into judgment, with every secret thing, whether good or evil.

"The whole duty of man" involves fearing the Lord. Spiritually speaking, the fear of the Lord stands in relationship to wisdom as the heart to the body, a foundation to a building, or a keel to a ship. FOL represents the alpha and the omega, the beginning and end of true wisdom. Without FOL, no true wisdom exists in an individual's life.

What does the fear of the Lord mean and how does it affect a person's life? FOL actually carries a bittersweet connotation. On one hand, there is the sweet awe, reverence, and submission to the Lord in whom a true believer delights because of his steadfast love (Ps 118:4). On the other hand, there is a proper dread and fear of God's response to sin and iniquity (Ps 119:120). God demands to be feared on the human level as one would fear the king (Ps 47:2)

---

4. Pss. 15:4; 19:9; 22:23, 25; 25:12, 14; 31:19; 33:8, 18; 34:7, 9, 11; 36:1; 47:2; 55:19; 60:4; 61:5; 66:16; 67:7; 72:5; 76:7, 11, 12; 85:9; 86:11; 89:7; 90:11; 96:4; 102:15; 103:11, 13, 17; 111:5, 10; 115:11, 13; 118:4; 119:63, 74, 79, 120; 128:1, 4; 130:4; 145:19; 147:11.

and on the divine level as the only true God (Ps 96:4–5). With reverent delight do true believers cultivate an appetite for the sweetness of his compassionate love which he promised forever in unlimited ways in response to obedience. By contrast, Christians shamefully accept the consequences of God's rebuke for their spiritual good (cf. Heb 12:3–11). This aspect represents the fear of God's retribution, especially dreadful for those who do not possess God's salvation.

The fear of the Lord proves to be more than just an Old Testament concept. You might be surprised to know that the fear of the Lord appears at least nineteen times in the New Testament (Matt 10:28; Luke 12:5; Acts 9:31; 10:2, 35; 13:16, 26; Rom 3:18; 2 Cor 5:11; 7:1; Eph 5:21; Phil 2:12; Col 3:22; Heb 10:31; 1 Peter 1:17; 2:17; Rev 11:18; 14:7; 19:5). From the Gospels, to Acts and the Epistles, and through Revelation, there runs a clearly discernible theme of fearing God. The basic teaching about FOL remains essentially the same in both Testaments.

Four kinds of people can be identified in relationship to the fear of the Lord. First, people who have no fear of God or the outcome of their sins (Rom 3:18; Rev 16:17–21). Second, people who fear the consequences of their sin, but reject God's redemption (Rom 13:3–5; Rev 6:15–17). Third, people who truly care about their sin, but without having a right relationship with God (Acts 10:2; 13:16, 26). Fourth, people who affectionately fear God because they are redeemed and because they care greatly about minimizing sin in their lives (Acts 10:35–36; 2 Cor 7:1). Only this last group has truly embraced Jesus Christ as Redeemer and Lord (Acts 16:30–31; Rom 10:9–13).

Now, before proceeding, let me ask, "At what level of fearing God are you?" If you are not in the fourth group, right now, right where you are, I lovingly urge you to repent of your sins and embrace the Lord Jesus Christ as your Savior. This is the wisest response to truth that you could ever make.

What else is important to know?

To help you further understand "wisdom's beginning," I have surveyed the theme of FOL, primarily in the Psalms and Proverbs with a "Question and Answer" format.

What does the fear of the Lord look like?

- Joyously delights in God's Word

Praise the LORD! Blessed is the man who fears the LORD,
who greatly delights in his commandments! (Ps 112:1)

- Consistently walks in God's way

Blessed is everyone who fears the LORD,
who walks in his ways! (Ps 128:1)

Whoever walks in uprightness fears the LORD,
but he who is devious in his ways despises him. (Prov 14:2)

The end of the matter; all has been heard. Fear God and keep his
commandments, for this is the whole duty of man. (Eccl 12:13)

- Boldly declares God's works

Then all mankind fears;
they tell what God has brought about
and ponder what he has done. (Ps 64:9)

- Patiently waits for God's reward

But the LORD takes pleasure in those who fear him,
in those who hope in his steadfast love. (Ps 147:11)

Why fear God?

- Christ commanded it

And do not fear those who kill the body but cannot kill the soul.
Rather fear him who can destroy both soul and body in hell. (Matt
10:28)

• Blessing is promised for it
Blessed is everyone who fears the LORD,
who walks in his ways! (Ps 128:1)

• Knowledge and wisdom are obtained from it
The fear of the LORD is the beginning of knowledge;
fools despise wisdom and instruction. (Prov 1:7)

The fear of the LORD is the beginning of wisdom,
and the knowledge of the Holy One is insight. (Prov 9:10)

• Judgment is rendered to those without it
The end of the matter; all has been heard. Fear God and keep his
commandments, for this is the whole duty of man. For God will bring
every deed into judgment, with every secret thing, whether good or
evil. (Eccl 12:13–14)

Who should fear God?

• All the inhabitants of the earth
Let all the earth fear the LORD;
let all the inhabitants of the world stand in awe of him! (Ps 33:8)

Where is the fear of the Lord found?

• Scripture
Confirm to your servant your promise,
that you may be feared. (Ps 119:38)

• Prayer
Teach me your way, O LORD, that I may walk in your truth;
unite my heart to fear your name. (Ps 86:11)

• Parents
Come, O children, listen to me;
I will teach you the fear of the LORD. (Ps 34:11)

How long should I fear God?

• Forever

Let not your heart envy sinners,
but continue in the fear of the LORD all the day. (Prov 23:17)

What are the benefits of fearing God?

• God's friendship

The friendship of the LORD is for those who fear him,
and he makes known to them his covenant. (Ps 25:14)

• God's goodness

Oh, how abundant is your goodness,
which you have stored up for those who fear you
and worked for those who take refuge in you,
in the sight of the children of mankind! (Ps 31:19)

• God's supply

Oh, fear the LORD, you his saints,
for those who fear him have no lack! (Ps 34:9)

• God's salvation

Surely his salvation is near to those who fear him,
that glory may dwell in our land. (Ps 85:9)

• God's fulfillment

He fulfills the desire of those who fear him;
he also hears their cry and saves them. (Ps 145:19)

• God's loving kindness

For as high as the heavens are above the earth,
so great is his steadfast love toward those who fear him; (Ps 103:11)

• God's increase

He will bless those who fear the LORD,

both the small and the great.
*May the L*ORD *give you increase,*
you and your children!
*May you be blessed by the L*ORD*,*
who made heaven and earth! (Ps 115:13–15)

• God's pleasure
*but the L*ORD *takes pleasure in those who fear him,*
in those who hope in his steadfast love. (Ps 147:11)

• God's instruction
*Who is the man who fears the L*ORD*?*
Him will he instruct in the way that he should choose. (Ps 25:12)

• God's knowledge
*The fear of the L*ORD *is the beginning of knowledge;*
fools despise wisdom and instruction. (Prov 1:7)

• God's understanding
*The fear of the L*ORD *is the beginning of wisdom;*
all those who practice it have a good understanding.
His praise endures forever! (Ps 111:10)

• God's wisdom
*The fear of the L*ORD *is the beginning of wisdom,*
and the knowledge of the Holy One is insight. (Prov 9:10)

• God's compassion
As a father shows compassion to his children,
*so the L*ORD *shows compassion to those who fear him. (Ps 103:13)*

• Longer life
*The fear of the L*ORD *prolongs life,*
but the years of the wicked will be short. (Prov 10:27)

- Avoidance of evil

By steadfast love and faithfulness iniquity is atoned for,
and by the fear of the LORD one turns away from evil. (Prov 16:6)

- Riches, honor, life

The reward for humility and fear of the LORD
is riches and honor and life. (Prov 22:4)

- Spiritual confidence

In the fear of the LORD one has strong confidence,
and his children will have a refuge. (Prov 14:26)

- Praise

Charm is deceitful, and beauty is vain,
but a woman who fears the LORD is to be praised. (Prov 31:30)

- Spiritual heritage

For you, O God, have heard my vows;
you have given me the heritage of those who fear your name. (Ps 61:5)

- God's blessing

Praise the LORD! Blessed is the man who fears the LORD,
who greatly delights in his commandments!
His offspring will be mighty in the land;
the generation of the upright will be blessed.
Wealth and riches are in his house,
and his righteousness endures forever.
Light dawns in the darkness for the upright;
he is gracious, merciful, and righteous.
It is well with the man who deals generously and lends;
who conducts his affairs with justice.
For the righteous will never be moved;
he will be remembered forever. (Ps 112:1–6)

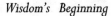

Now having thoroughly examined "wisdom's beginning" – the fear of the Lord, – plunge ahead to learn about "Lady Wisdom" (Prov 8:1–36) in all her splendor and glory.

4

WISDOM'S WIND[5]

Having previously been a United States' naval officer, I was delighted one afternoon to find *A Sailor's Dictionary* while browsing through a favorite bookstore. The dust jacket read, "A dictionary for landlubbers, old salts and armchair drifters." It sounded inviting.

Intrigued, I picked up the book to sample the humor. It described sailing as: "The fine art of getting wet and becoming ill while slowly going nowhere at great expense." It later struck me – that is true not only of sailing but also of the spiritual life, unless we are propelled through life by the gentle breeze of God's transforming wisdom.

That observation raises the question, "How can wisdom's wind fill the sails of my life so that the journey will be safe and I ultimately arrive at the destination of God's choice?" The following discussion about wisdom, fueled by various Scriptures, answers this significant spiritual question.

Wisdom's source

Wisdom cries aloud in the street, in the markets she raises her voice; at the head of the noisy streets she cries out; at the

5. This chapter has been adapted and expanded from Richard Mayhue, "Transformed by God's Wisdom," in *Seeking God: How to Develop an Intimate Spiritual Relationship* (Fearn, Ross-shire, Great Britain: Christian Focus, 2000), 121–128.

entrance of the city gates she speaks: How long, O simple ones, will you love being simple? How long will scoffers delight in their scoffing and fools hate knowledge? If you turn at my reproof, behold, I will pour out my spirit to you; I will make my words known to you. Because I have called and you refused to listen, have stretched out my hand and no one has heeded, because you have ignored all my counsel and would have none of my reproof, I also will laugh at your calamity; I will mock when terror strikes you, when terror strikes you like a storm and your calamity comes like a whirlwind, when distress and anguish come upon you. Then they will call upon me, but I will not answer; they will seek me diligently but will not find me. Because they hated knowledge and did not choose the fear of the Lord, would have none of my counsel and despised all my reproof, therefore they shall eat the fruit of their way, and have their fill of their own devices. For the simple are killed by their turning away, and the complacency of fools destroys them; but whoever listens to me will dwell secure and will be at ease, without dread of disaster. (Prov 1:20–33)

The writer of Proverbs puts wisdom in street language. Figuratively portrayed as a woman crying out in the city, wisdom beckons the people to turn from their sinful scoffing to God's reproof and its attendant reward (vv. 23, 33).

Jesus parallels this same idea with his "Parable of the Two Builders."

Everyone then who hears these words of mine and does them will be like a wise man who built his house on the rock. And the rain fell, and the floods came, and the winds blew and beat on that house, but it did not fall, because it had been founded on the rock. And everyone who hears these words of mine and does not do them will be like a foolish man who built his house on the sand. And the rain fell, and the floods came, and the winds blew and beat against that house, and it fell, and great was the fall of it. (Matt 7:24–27)

Your spiritual transformation began when you received Jesus Christ as Savior and Lord. Paul describes him as the one "in whom are hidden all the treasures of wisdom and knowledge" (Col 2:3; see 1 Cor 1:24, 30). God's gift, his Spirit, comes to indwell believers with what Isaiah calls "The spirit of wisdom and understanding, the spirit of counsel and might, the spirit of knowledge and the fear of the Lord" (Isa 11:2). Paul reminds everyone that the one to whom glory will be given forever is "the only wise God" (Rom 16:27), referring to God the Father. Therefore, your relationship to Father, Son, and Holy Spirit refers to a union with pure wisdom. Thus, your transformation comes by the personal presence and power of divine wisdom in your life. Only by the gracious, divine transformation of sinners can anyone hope to "practice" the wisdom of Proverbs.

Wisdom's manner

God's will, his Word, and his way are all wise. Everything about God is wise; all else is foolishness. The following short biblical catechism answers several key questions about wisdom.

Where can wisdom be found?

> The law of the Lord is perfect, reviving the soul; the testimony of the Lord is sure, making wise the simple. (Ps 19:7)

> But as for you, continue in what you have learned and have firmly believed, knowing from whom you learned it and how from childhood you have been acquainted with the sacred writings, which are able to make you wise for salvation through faith in Christ Jesus. (2 Tim 3:14–15)

What identifies true wisdom?

> The fear of the Lord is the beginning of wisdom; all those who practice it have a good understanding. His praise endures forever! (Ps 111:10)

The fear of the Lord is the beginning of wisdom, and the knowledge of the Holy One is insight. (Prov 9:10)

How valuable is wisdom?

Blessed is the one who finds wisdom, and the one who gets understanding, for the gain from her is better than gain from silver and her profit better than gold. She is more precious than jewels, and nothing you desire can compare with her. Long life is in her right hand; in her left hand are riches and honor. Her ways are ways of pleasantness, and all her paths are peace. She is a tree of life to those who lay hold of her; those who hold her fast are called blessed. (Prov 3:13–18)

How is wisdom obtained?

If any of you lacks wisdom, let him ask God, who gives generously to all without reproach, and it will be given him. But let him ask in faith, with no doubting, for the one who doubts is like a wave of the sea that is driven and tossed by the wind. For that person must not suppose that he will receive anything from the Lord; he is a double-minded man, unstable in all his ways. (James 1:5–8)

Are there any warnings about wisdom?

Thus says the LORD: "Let not the wise man boast in his wisdom, let not the mighty man boast in his might, let not the rich man boast in his riches, but let him who boasts boast in this, that he understands and knows me, that I am the LORD who practices steadfast love, justice, and righteousness in the earth. For in these things I delight, declares the LORD." (Jer 9:23–24)

Are there any surprises with wisdom?

> Let no one deceive himself. If anyone among you thinks that
> he is wise in this age, let him become a fool that he may
> become wise. (1 Cor 3:18)

What should be done with wisdom?

> Look carefully then how you walk, not as unwise but as wise,
> making the best use of the time, because the days are evil.
> Therefore do not be foolish, but understand what the will of
> the Lord is. (Eph 5:15–17)

Wisdom's fruit

> Who is wise and understanding among you? By his good
> conduct let him show his works in the meekness of wisdom.
> But if you have bitter jealousy and selfish ambition in your
> hearts, do not boast and be false to the truth. This is not the
> wisdom that comes down from above, but is earthly,
> unspiritual, demonic. For where jealousy and selfish ambition
> exist, there will be disorder and every vile practice. But the
> wisdom from above is first pure, then peaceable, gentle, open
> to reason, full of mercy and good fruits, impartial and sincere.
> And a harvest of righteousness is sown in peace by those who
> make peace. (James 3:13–18)

James distinguishes between an earthly wisdom and true godly
wisdom from above. Wisdom from God will reflect good conduct
with a gentle character, while the counterfeit wisdom of demons or
mere humans produces evil and disorder. Righteousness and peace
accompany authentic wisdom. In verse 17, a kaleidoscope of
wisdom's qualities describes the transformed life of one who is
spiritually mature. James asks, "Who among you is wise and
understanding?" in verse 13, and then provides the basis for

determining the answer in verse 17. Eight characteristics of wisdom authenticate true godly wisdom.

Pure. The premier feature of godly wisdom involves cleanness or, put another way, the absence of sin's pollution. Wisdom and a desire for sinlessness are synonymous. The church should be pure like a chaste virgin (2 Cor 11:2); Christians need to think on pure things (Phil 4:8); young women are to be pure (Titus 2:5); and leaders in the church need to keep pure (1 Tim 5:22).

The ancient church father Tertullian (ca. AD 160–215) put purity in perspective with his statement:

> Be clothed with the silk of honesty, the fine linen of holiness and the purple of chastity; thus adorned, God will be your friend.

As Christ wisely withstood the impure lure of sin, so should you (Matt. 4:1–11). Therefore, all wisdom of God will be morally and ethically spotless and in keeping with God's attribute of holiness.

Peaceable. Wisdom makes peace, not war. Peacemakers are called sons of God (Matt 5:9). Peaceful unity is encouraged (Ps 133). Peace appears among the fruit produced by God's Spirit (Gal 5:22). You are to let the peace of Christ rule your hearts (Col 3:15; Phil 4:7). Since Christ is called the Prince of Peace (Isa 9:6), Christians should be ambassadors of peace (2 Cor 5:20). Christians are called to be at peace with others (Rom 12:18). Take the way of peace as the best route to travel on your journey through life.

Gentle. The Greek word translated 'gentle' contains much more than the English word conveys. Let me try to amplify it with some descriptive phrases:
- sweet reasonableness
- going the second mile
- not demanding one's rights

- full of mercy
- discerning between the letter and spirit of the law

Gentleness should characterize the elders' behavior in the church (1 Tim 3:3). Believers need to be gentle with one another (Phil 4:5). Ultimately, Christians are to be gentle with all people (Titus 3:2). As Christ wisely spoke gentle words to the thief, so should you to those who seek Christ (Luke 23:39–43). You are like the Savior when you exhibit the wisdom of gentleness (2 Cor 10:1). In so doing, anger, a retaliatory spirit, and running over people will not be a part of the wise person's life at any time.

Reasonable. Wisdom makes you conciliatory and willing to yield when spiritual progress can be gained. If you are reasonable, no one will ever characterize you as "coarse grade" sandpaper. Christ always yielded to his Heavenly Father. Reasonableness does not compromise truth, but rather recognizes another's idea as important when dealing with non-absolutes.

I can do nothing on my own. As I hear, I judge, and my judgment is just, because I seek not my own will but the will of him who sent me. (John 5:30)

Full of mercy. Since God is rich in mercy, so should you be (Eph 2:4). By God's great mercy, you were born again and made heirs of eternal life (Titus 3:5; 1 Peter 1:3). Mercy withholds judgment and extends grace without violating justice. You can follow in the footsteps of Christ's full mercy, as extended to the harlot (John 8:1–11) and to Peter (John 21:17). This wise love covers a multitude of sins (Prov 10:12; James 5:20; 1 Peter 4:8).

Full of good fruits. This feature is not so much about fruit in character as it is about fruit in action that qualifies to be called good. Like mercy, these fruits should flow in abundance. The pattern that James establishes follows the teaching of Jesus who demanded fruit (John 15:2), *more* fruit (John 15:2), and *much* fruit (John 15:5,8).

This explains one major reason why God saved people – for good works (Eph 2:10).

Unwavering. With regard to the things of God, Christians are to be single-minded, without compromise, without partiality, and always consistent. If you are solidly anchored by the truth, you won't be blown around by every wind of doctrine or trickery of men (Eph 4:14). Neither will you be doubleminded (James 1:6–8). Like Christ, you should always pray,

> Father, if you are willing, remove this cup from me. Nevertheless, not my will, but yours, be done. (Luke 22:42)

Without hypocrisy. Sincere, genuine, unpretentious, and "without a mask" all describe this quality. Your love (Rom 12:9) and your faith (1 Tim 1:5) are to be without hypocrisy. What you claim to be, you are to be. Just as Jesus claimed to be a servant (Matt 20:28) and actually served (John 13:12–17), so you need to live with transparent honesty. Your life should be an open book which can be read at any time by anyone.

Wisdom's transformation

Job twice asks the significant question: "Where can wisdom be found; where does wisdom come from?" (Job 28:12, 20). He answers his own questions,

> God understands the way to it, and he knows its place. For he looks to the ends of the earth and sees everything under the heavens. When he gave to the wind its weight and apportioned the waters by measure, when he made a decree for the rain and a way for the lightning of the thunder, then he saw it and declared it; he established it, and searched it out. And he said to man, "Behold, the fear of the Lord, that is wisdom, and to turn away from evil is understanding." (Job 28:23–28)

Wisdom begins with repentance and the transformation wrought by salvation, but it does not end there. Wisdom resides in God's Word (Ps 19:7). By it, believers are transformed through the renewing of their minds (Rom 12:2). Going a step further, wisdom not only knows God's Word, but also obeys it.

> The end of the matter; all has been heard. Fear God and keep his commandments, for this is the whole duty of man. (Eccl 12:13)

True wisdom avoids being conformed to this world and its lusts (Rom 12:2; 1 Peter 1:14), and pursues transformation into the image of our wise Savior.

> And we all, with unveiled face, beholding the glory of the Lord, are being transformed into the same image from one degree of glory to another. For this comes from the Lord who is the Spirit. (2 Cor 3:18)

Wisdom's acquisition

For a true Christian, authentic spiritual wisdom can be gained in at least four ways. First, you can ask God for wisdom. When Solomon could have had anything he wanted from God, he requested wisdom and discernment (1 Kings 3:3–9). God commended him because he did not seek long life or riches, but wisdom. Thus, Solomon became the wisest man in history (1 Kings 4:29–34). This same invitation to pray for wisdom awaits you today.

> If any of you lacks wisdom, let him ask God, who gives generously to all without reproach, and it will be given him. But let him ask in faith, with no doubting, for the one who doubts is like a wave of the sea that is driven and tossed by the wind. For that person must not suppose that he will receive anything from the Lord; he is a double-minded man, unstable in all his ways. (James 1:5–8)

Second, wisdom can also be obtained from God's Word (Ps. 119:98–100). God's invitation to partake of the trustworthy Scriptures remains available to all.

Let the Word of Christ dwell in you richly. (Col 3:16)

Third, wisdom closely associates itself with the Holy Spirit. God filled Bezalel with the Spirit of God in wisdom (Ex 31:3) as He did the seven servants of the early church (Acts 6:3). Thus, to be filled with the Holy Spirit means to be controlled by wisdom.

Fourth, the crowds marveled at Christ's wisdom (Matt 13:54; Mark 6:2). Luke reports that Jesus increased in wisdom (2:40, 52). Thus, as you abide in him (John 15:4–7), you abide in wisdom.

Christian spirituality involves growing to be like God in character and conduct through *the transforming work and wisdom* of God's Word and God's Spirit.

Five kinds of fools

In radical contrast to the above discussion about wisdom, the Bible also teaches much about foolishness. Scripture defines five kinds of fools and asserts that every living person is a fool of some kind. Take a careful look at your life. What kind of fool are you?

First Fool (Pss 14:1; 53:1). This person announces, "There is no God," and blatantly denies the existence of God. He/she is the Madelyn Murray O'Hare of my generation, or the Robert Ingersoll (1833–1899) of days past. The infamous agnostic one day publicly shook his fist at God and demanded, "If you are real, strike me dead, and I give you thirty seconds to do it." Then, he arrogantly got his watch out and timed God. At the end of 30 seconds, he looked skyward and he said, "God, You don't exist."

I do not know to whom he was speaking, and neither did he. Ingersoll's logic proved to be problematic because, if God did not exist, he was addressing no one. With this illogical challenge, he evidenced an even greater personal problem. He was a fool, according to the Word of God, because the fool has said in his heart, "There is no God."

Second Fool (1 Cor 1:18). This fool rejects the cross of Christ. "For the word of the cross is folly to those who are perishing, but to us who are being saved it is the power of God." The world bulges with religions that absolutely reject the reality of the cross, and even deny its historical existence. Christ's death represents the furthest thing from their minds when they think of having a right relationship with God, much less his resurrection. Paul concludes this to be foolishness because these people will utterly perish.

Third Fool (Matt 7:26–27). This fool disobeys God's Word with respect to salvation. This person when asked, "Do you believe in a living God?" might say, "Sure I do, don't you?" Literally hundreds of thousands of people, even millions, in the world will glibly affirm the existence of God and the reality of the cross, but are still going to hell because they base their salvation on something other than Christ's substitutionary death. Matthew 7:24–27 contrasts the wise and the foolish builders. Violent and destructive storms came on both of them; one house stood, the other fell. Why? Because the foolish builder failed to follow the clear Word of God with respect to salvation, but the wise builder obeyed.

Fourth Fool (Luke 24:25). This fool fails to believe all of God's Word. The resurrected Christ, while walking on the road to Emmaus, met up with two disciples pouring out their hearts in grief that the Christ had been crucified, and that their hopes of him being Messiah were dashed. Jesus appropriately responded to these dear men, distraught over his death, and doubting his promised resurrection. "O foolish ones, and slow of heart to believe all that the prophets have spoken!" You are also fools, like them, if you fail to believe and appropriate all that the prophets have written.

Fifth Fool (1 Cor 4:10). In distinct contrast to the previous kinds of fools, only this variation receives God's commendation. This fool lives life wholeheartedly for Christ's sake. Paul announced to the Corinthians, "We are fools for Christ's sake." If you want to be a fool, this is the kind to be. Be a fool for Christ's sake. Being this kind of fool always causes God's wisdom to manifest itself in your life. This kind of fool honors and glorifies God, seeking to please him in all things.

Have you made the wise choice of being this fifth kind of fool? If so, the sails of your life will always be filled with the winds of God's wisdom. Now, proceed to discover that you have made the right choice because **Wisdom's Way Is Best**.

5

WISDOM'S WAY IS BEST

Look around our world. Read the theological, philosophical, and historical literature of the day. Then realize that those who occupy the most prestigious seats of academia are telling you that the world has abandoned the era of rational, objective thought, and is rapidly affirming personal opinion and relativism as the superior guide for life.

Philosophers term this convoluted way of thinking "postmodernism." Historians call it "revisionism." This approach basically involves setting aside the factuality of life and accepting only whatever one thinks is or ought to be reality, whether it squares with the facts of life or not. This new mindset abandons anything absolute and exalts what is relative. Therefore, everyone is supposedly right and, apparently, no one can be wrong.

Sin is paraded around as nothing more than "sickness"; drug consumption is spoken of as "recreation"; the traditional family is considered to be an outdated, endangered species. Evil is labeled as good. Immorality is heralded as "sexual freedom." Pornography is projected as "freedom of speech." Homosexuality is defined as an "alternative lifestyle." Abortion is sugar-coated by calling it "post-conception birth control"; and lawlessness is condoned as "liberation."

This faulty worldview[6] raises the critical question "What are the absolutes, if there are any?" Which values, which morals, or which ethics should you embrace to give you the most righteous, peaceful, and fruitful life possible? Thinking by comparison in the moral realm, you might ask what ranks with the certainty of the law of gravity or the laws of thermodynamics?

To whom should you give your attention? Would it be Plato or Aristotle, the ancient philosophers? Cicero or Confucius? In the more modern history of America, Will Rogers or Mark Twain? And in even more recent days, Bill Bennett who wrote *The Book of Virtues*? What book, what philosopher, what moralist should you look to for guidance on how best to live your life?

You must ultimately turn to the Scriptures, God-breathed and inerrant, proclaiming the voice and the mind of God, to find the kind of wisdom that a world which is blind to the truth desperately needs, but believes it has already embraced. So, you can look at Proverbs as God's most concentrated presentation of wisdom – wisdom that is concrete and immediately applicable, not theoretical. I hope this will be a pre-eminently practical chapter on a theme that I have not found developed elsewhere – "the better way" of Proverbs.

Proverbs supplies "wisdom" to those who are less than fully wise, "understanding" to those who haven't yet gotten a firm grip on life. To the best educated person and the smallest child, it has much to offer. Proverbs' basic theme, summed up in one sentence, would be: The fear of the Lord leads to divine wisdom for righteous living. (1:7; 3:5; 9:10; 22:4).

All kinds of questions and dilemmas in life – whether in the marketplace, or within yourself, or in your relationship with God – are addressed in the book of Proverbs. There, you will find very real, down-to-earth, tangible, righteous answers which, if followed, will bring great pleasure and glory to God, not to mention peace and hope in your own life.

6. For a thorough discussion of "worldview," see John MacArthur, Richard L. Mayhue, and John A. Hughes, eds. *Think Biblically! Recovering A Christian Worldview*: Wheaton, IL: Crossway, 2003.

Of all the commentaries written on the book of Proverbs, one of the two[7] that I prefer was penned in the 19th century by Charles Bridges – 1846 to be exact. About Proverbs (pp.xii–xiii), he writes:

Nor is it only a mirror to show our defects. It is also a guidebook and a directory for godly conduct....Beside a code of laws directly religious, a variety of admirable rules stream forth from the deep recesses of wisdom and spread over the whole field. All ranks and classes have their word in season. The Sovereign on the throne is instructed as from God. The principles of national prosperity or decay are laid open. The rich are warned of their besetting temptations. The poor are cheered in their worldly humiliation. Wise rules are given for self-government. It bridles the injurious tongue, corrects the wanton eye, and ties the unjust hand in chains. It prevents sloth; chastises all absurd desires; teaches prudence; raises man's courage and represents temperance and chastity after such a fashion, that we cannot but have them in veneration. To come to important matters so often mismanaged – the blessing or curse of the marriage ordinance is vividly portrayed. Sound principles of family order and discipline are inculcated. Domestic economy is displayed in its adorning consistency. Nay – even the minute courtesies of daily life are regulated. Self-denying consideration of others, and liberal distribution are enforced....Thus if the Psalms bring the glow upon the heart, the Proverbs "make the face to shine."

Proverbs, without question, stands as the family manual by which fathers and mothers are to nurture and guide their sons and daughters. Decidedly, one should disciple a new believer in Proverbs. And, recently for me, it has been the book with which a grandfather can disciple his grandsons.

---

7. The other one is Peter A. Steveson, *A Commentary on Proverbs*.

Proverbs covers all aspects of life, whether it is your personal life, your spiritual life, your relationship with God, your family life, your relationship with your spouse and your children, your school life, your community life, or your workplace life. It is, quite practically, a guide to glorifying God by living wisely.

Proverbs will instruct you on how to be blessed by God; as you have read in Chapter 3, it tells you what the fear of the Lord looks like and how to live it out. It talks about life and death, prayer and sacrifice. Proverbs discusses reward, righteousness, sin, anger, humility, love, hate, lying, morality, what you ought to do and what you should not do when speaking. It talks about authority, accountability, correction, marriage, and parenting. Any and everything you would possibly want to know in terms of how to live in a way that would be pleasing to God is addressed – integrity, loyalty, truth, wealth, benevolence, friendship, your reputation, etc.

Over the years, one special theme in Proverbs has especially intrigued me more than others – "the better way." This idea involves the Hebrew adjective which is translated "better." It is used in a comparative sense – "this way is better than that way." But, you will discover from the context (wisdom compared to foolishness), the comparative actually becomes a superlative, which means, "this way is the very best way," i.e. the Christian way.

Ten priorities emerge from twenty-one passages that promote "the better way," which ultimately proves to be the best way.

1. Wisdom or wealth?

Number one encompasses the over-arching theme of wealth contrasted with wisdom. Which one should be the top priority? Proverbs leaves no doubt about the answer.

> Blessed is the one who finds wisdom, and the one who gets understanding, for the gain from her is better than gain from silver and her profit better than gold. (Prov 3:13–14)

> For wisdom is better than jewels, and all that you may desire cannot compare with her. (Prov 8:11)

> My fruit is better than gold, even fine gold, and my yield than choice silver. (Prov 8:19)

> How much better to get wisdom than gold! To get understanding is to be chosen rather than silver. (Prov 16:16)

Some of the most godly people throughout church history have been people of poverty; but they also have often been people whose lives were cut short by martyrdom because of their selfless testimony for the Lord Jesus Christ, like the church of Smyrna (Rev 2:8–11).

Wisdom is always preferable over wealth, without even a second thought, because, "Christ...[is] the wisdom of God" (1 Cor 1:24). Colossians 2:3 says that it is Christ "...in whom are hidden all the treasures of wisdom and knowledge." Wisdom supplies spiritual wealth, a superior asset. Wisdom points to Christ. Wisdom urges people to embrace Christ and all that is his. After you have received Christ as your all in all, you can allow God to decide at what level or what lifestyle you are going to live. Acquiring wisdom, not wealth, should be your passion.

When I was attending seminary, the only savings our little family had was already spoken for to pay tuition. We lived hand to mouth, week to week, month after month, on my monthly wages of about $400. We never had much, but we never had too little. And, I can remember envying some of my classmates whose clothes were far better than mine, who owned libraries that were much larger than my own, and who had cars that didn't look junky like ours.

As a seminary student, I quickly had to deal with the reality of encroaching envy and materialism. Finally, I concluded that I needed to thank God for the way he had blessed those other men. It was right for me to thank God that they had a better car, they had a bigger library, or they dressed in nicer clothes. Then, I needed to thank God for what he had given to me. I also repented from the sins of envy and covetousness.

Proverbs teaches that the wisest approach lets him choose the course of your life with regard to money. The better way of wisdom always exceeds wealth in God's economy.

2. Humility or pride?

The second "better way" appears in Proverbs 12:9:

> Better to be lowly and have a servant than to play the great man and lack bread.

This proverb contrasts visible poverty with invisible prosperity. It speaks to the vanity of appearance, about someone who wants to look successful even though a fake or charade. For example, the attitude of "appearance for appearance's sake" undoubtedly is a major factor in driving up the astronomically high credit card debt in America.

These people want to be seen driving the right car; their house is fully decorated; they are always fashionably dressed for every occasion; and they seem to have everything that borrowed money can buy. Appearance to them is everything. But, it is "better to be of a lowly spirit with the poor than to divide the spoil with the proud." (Prov 16:19).

Proverbs 25:7 says that:

> It is better to be told "Come up here," than to be put lower in the presence of a noble.

The right road will always be the one of humility. It is the path of "the back seat," of the servant. Places and times exist in life where you will be conscious of rank or status. So, what should you seek? Proverbs would counsel: Better to sit in the back row and have the person who is leading the meeting call you to the front, than to sit on the front row and embarrass him and yourself when he asks you to move back. Read Luke 14:7–11 and you will discover that the Lord Jesus taught this principle also.

The way of wisdom involves the way of humility, not the way of pride.

3. The fear of the Lord or not?

Better is a little with the fear of the Lord than great treasure and trouble with it. (Prov 15:16)

Before being saved, I possessed a great deal. Because of my promising naval career, people said I would be a tremendous success. And yet, I was on my way to hell and didn't even know it. My crumbling marriage impatiently anticipated the certainty of divorce. I had a form of prosperity, but without the fear of the Lord. Let me tell you, I would never want to regain that prosperity with its accompanying trouble, only to lose what I now have in Jesus Christ. Poverty with the fear of the Lord is the way to go. It is the better way, absolutely the best way.

4. Love or hate?

Better is a dinner of herbs where love is than a fattened ox and hatred with it. (Prov 15:17)

It is far better to live in an environment of love, even if you have nothing else, than to live in a mansion, to have multiple cars, and to possess a luxurious life accompanied by hate.

You will encounter people who have far more than you have, and far more than probably most of the people in your church possess. But, unless they are true Christians, they have one desperate need – to know Jesus Christ as their Savior. Without him, they belong to the most impoverished people-group alive, although for a moment they appear to be the richest.

When their eyes are opened to their sin, and they recognize the pain of their iniquity, they would gladly trade their prosperity and the hatefulness that usually goes along with it, to live a humble life, to know something of the love of God, and to have the ability to love others as they have been loved.

Love is always the better way.

5. Righteousness or injustice?

Better is a little with righteousness than great revenues with injustice. (Prov 16:8)

Prosperity and poverty have been contrasted in these last three opposites: Prosperity without the fear of the Lord, prosperity with hate, and prosperity with pride; or, put positively – poverty with the fear of the Lord, poverty with love, and poverty with humility.

What does the foolish flesh want to worry about? It seeks to fret about wealth and to be anxious about prosperity. So, you must recommit yourself on a daily basis to the better way. You must inseparably join yourself to wisdom as opposed to wealth, humility rather than pride, the fear of the Lord in contrast to prosperity, love not hate, and righteousness rather than injustice. This is the better way.

6. Peace or anger?

Whoever is slow to anger is better than the mighty, and he who rules his spirit than he who takes a city. (Prov 16:32)

Proverbs 17:1 advises, "Better is a dry morsel with quiet than a house full of feasting with strife." Being slow to anger is a far superior quality than being a hot tempered, aggressive person who can conquer nations. Better merely to have a crust of bread but a peaceful home, than to own a grocery store but feast at home with strife, anger, and turmoil. Peace along with a simple life will always be much more highly prized than anger with power and prestige.

If you are driven by any of the less important options in features one to five, then the power and the prestige that you foolishly crave will almost always be accomplished by anger and injustice. Selfishly, you may cheat people out of what is rightfully theirs, so that you can pompously parade yourself as someone who is wealthy and prosperous. But that is all a deceptive façade that will sooner or later vanish.

Just the opposite approach ought to characterize a Christian's life. Choose peace – the better way.

7. Integrity or deceitfulness?

Here is a seventh choice to ponder in Proverbs' continuing contrast between two ways of living.

Better is a poor person who walks in his integrity than one who is crooked in speech and is a fool. (Prov 19:1)

A good name is to be chosen rather than great riches, and favor is better than silver or gold. (Prov 22:1)

Better is a poor man who walks in his integrity than a rich man who is crooked in his ways. (Prov 28:6)

Proverbs 19:22 proposes that it is better to be "a poor man...than a liar." Poverty with truth and integrity proves noble and dignified, in contrast to a foolish prosperity with deceitfulness and dishonesty. This principle can influence everything from the way you pay your bills or prepare your taxes, to the way you treat people. Poverty with truth and integrity is an honest, preferred way to live, for which no one ought to make excuses or feel a need to make an apology. God most highly values inward character, not outward appearance (cf. 1 Sam 16:7). Integrity always will be the better way.

8. A loving or a contentious wife?

This next "better way" needs to capture every married couple's attention.

These three proverbs say essentially the same thing and use similar language.

> It's better to live in a corner of the housetop than in a house shared with a quarrelsome wife. (Prov 21:9)

> It is better to live in a desert land than with a quarrelsome and fretful woman. (Prov 21:19)

> It is better to live in a corner of the housetop than in a house shared with a quarrelsome wife. (Prov 25:24)

A humble but happy home is the wise way to go, in contrast to a prosperous home with a contentious woman. I doubt if a man ever got married because the one who was the object of his affections wanted to argue all the time. Rarely does that happen – it turns out to be incredibly unwise and unpleasant. You do have a choice. Know what the woman whom you might marry is like during stressful times, or when she doesn't always get her way.

Unfortunately, many contentious Christian wives that I have counseled are women who have been ill-treated – not abused physically, but just ill-treated by neglect, and frustrated by husbands who will not assume the proper biblical role and exercise the right spiritual responsibilities that are laid down in the Word of God. Some husbands have not chosen "the better way," and thus may be part of the problem.

These women have not been loved by their husbands as Christ loved the church and gave Himself for her. In other words, husbands are not sacrificing themselves for the sake of their wives. While this does not excuse unbiblical behavior on the wife's part, it does put the husband on notice that he needs to treat his wife in a Scriptural manner. Together, they need to pursue the better way of love.

9. Love – expressed or suppressed?

Better is open rebuke than hidden love. (Prov 27:5)

Expressed love, even though by way of wisely offered criticism, is far better than suppressed love, i.e. never spoken or demonstrated. Proverbs 13:24 puts it this way with regard to your children, "He who spares his rod hates his son, but he who loves him disciplines him diligently."

What does Solomon mean by that? Why is spanking on the verge of being outlawed in many parts of our country? Because society has decided that corporal punishment properly applied represents an act of what? Hate and abuse, not an act of love. In contrast, the Bible says it defines an act of love. And hate involves withholding the kind of discipline that would bring godliness and reward to a child.

A similar statement appears in 28:23, "Whoever rebukes a man will afterward find more favor than he who flatters with his tongue." If you deal with someone in a reputable, honest way, although it might be in a negative context momentarily, this is far better than dealing with someone who schmoozes you for what they can get out of the situation, not for what you can receive from them.

Expressed love, even in rebuke, is always far better than never-expressed or suppressed love.

10. Faithful or undependable?

Do not forsake your friend and your father's friend, and do not go to your brother's house in the day of your calamity. Better is a neighbor who is near than a brother who is far away. (Prov 27:10)

Faithfulness in relationships is far better than not being dependable. This could be taken in two ways. One is a *geographical* way. If your family lives on the east coast and you live in the West, you are probably far better off in a time of immediate need, to depend on some helpful person who lives in the same apartment building or neighborhood.

Its ultimate intent, however, is *relational*. Better is a neighbor who is committed to you personally, than a family member who is not. Some have been abandoned by their family because they refuse to reject Jesus Christ. Perhaps your natural family disinherited you, or put you at arm's length, or will do nothing to help you because of your faith relationship with the Lord Jesus. However, God has provided Christian brothers and sisters in the church who will be dependable, because being faithful is the better way.

Final thoughts

I personally became very excited upon first recognizing these wise principles. During the discovery process, it dawned on me that in my short time on earth I could live in the very best way possible. Put in ordinary language, "It doesn't get any better than this." The wise way of Proverbs is always the best way – now and forevermore – in all of life's relationships.

The same is true for parents. Proverbs overflows with biblical advice on wise parenting. You can make no greater investment at the earliest age possible for your children than to regularly read and meditate on Proverbs as a family. Here is a sample of ten "starter" principles from Proverbs as outlined by my special friend in life and in ministry, John MacArthur (*Successful Christian Parenting*, 77–104).

1. Teach your children to fear the Lord (Prov 1:7; 9:10).
2. Teach your children to guard their minds (Prov 4:23).
3. Teach your children to obey their parents (Prov 1:8).
4. Teach your children how to select their companions (Prov 13:20).
5. Teach your children to control their lusts (Prov 2:16–19; 5:3–5).
6. Teach your children to enjoy their spouses (Prov 5:15–20).
7. Teach your children to watch their words (Prov 4:24).
8. Teach your children to pursue their work (Prov 6:6–8).
9. Teach your children to manage their money (Prov 3:9–10).
10. Teach your children to love their neighbors (Prov 3:27–29).

Well, enough *about* Proverbs – now it's time to *embrace* Proverbs, all 915 verses of God's eternal wisdom. I pray that your spiritual appetite has been whetted by reading these introductory chapters like a menu and that you are now ready to feast on the actual biblical meal that will nourish your soul to live wisely for God's glory by habitually practicing Proverbs.

6

SPIRITUAL WISDOM

Abomination

3:32   For the devious person is an abomination to the Lord, but the upright are in his confidence.

6:16–19   There are six things that the Lord hates, seven that are an abomination to him: haughty eyes, a lying tongue, and hands that shed innocent blood, a heart that devises wicked plans, feet that make haste to run to evil, a false witness who breathes out lies, and one who sows discord among brothers.

8:7   For my mouth will utter truth; wickedness is an abomination to my lips.

11:1   A false balance is an abomination to the Lord, but a just weight is his delight.

11:20   Those of crooked heart are an abomination to the Lord, but those of blameless ways are his delight.

12:22   Lying lips are an abomination to the Lord, but those who act faithfully are his delight.

13:19   A desire fulfilled is sweet to the soul, but to turn away from evil is an abomination to fools.

15:8–9   The sacrifice of the wicked is an abomination to the Lord, but the prayer of the upright is acceptable to him. The way of the wicked is an abomination to the Lord, but he loves him who pursues righteousness.

15:26   The thoughts of the wicked are an abomination to the Lord, but gracious words are pure.

16:5   Everyone who is arrogant in heart is an abomination to the Lord; be assured, he will not go unpunished.

16:12   It is an abomination to kings to do evil, for the throne is established by righteousness.

17:15   He who justifies the wicked and he who condemns the righteous are both alike an abomination to the Lord.

20:10   Unequal weights and unequal measures are both alike an abomination to the Lord.

20:23   Unequal weights are an abomination to the Lord, and false scales are not good.

21:27   The sacrifice of the wicked is an abomination; how much more when he brings it with evil intent.

24:8–9   Whoever plans to do evil will be called a schemer. The devising of folly is sin, and the scoffer is an abomination to mankind.

26:24–25   Whoever hates disguises himself with his lips and harbors deceit in his heart; when he speaks graciously, believe him not, for there are seven abominations in his heart.

28:9   If one turns away his ear from hearing the law, even his prayer is an abomination.

29:27   An unjust man is an abomination to the righteous, but one whose way is straight is an abomination to the wicked.

Blessing/Favor

3:13   Blessed is the one who finds wisdom, and the one who gets understanding.

3:33   The Lord's curse is on the house of the wicked, but he blesses the dwelling of the righteous.

5:18   Let your fountain be blessed, and rejoice in the wife of your youth.

8:32   And now, O sons, listen to me: blessed are those who keep my ways.

8:34   Blessed is the one who listens to me, watching daily at my gates, waiting beside my doors.

8:35–36   For whoever finds me finds life and obtains favor from the Lord, but he who fails to find me injures himself; all who hate me love death.

10:6–7   Blessings are on the head of the righteous, but the mouth of the wicked conceals violence. The memory of the righteous is a blessing, but the name of the wicked will rot.

10:22   The blessing of the Lord makes rich, and he adds no sorrow with it.

11:11   By the blessing of the upright a city is exalted, but by the mouth of the wicked it is overthrown.

11:26   The people curse him who holds back grain, but a blessing is on the head of him who sells it.

12:2   A good man obtains favor from the Lord, but a man of evil devices he condemns.

16:20   Whoever gives thought to the word will discover good, and blessed is he who trusts in the Lord.

18:22   He who finds a wife finds a good thing and obtains favor from the Lord.

20:7   The righteous who walks in his integrity – blessed are his children after him!

20:21   An inheritance gained hastily in the beginning will not be blessed in the end.

22:9   Whoever has a bountiful eye will be blessed, for he shares his bread with the poor.

24:25   But those who rebuke the wicked will have delight, and a good blessing will come upon them.

28:14   Blessed is the one who fears the Lord always, but whoever hardens his heart will fall into calamity.

28:20   A faithful man will abound with blessings, but whoever hastens to be rich will not go unpunished.

29:18   Where there is no prophetic vision the people cast off restraint, but blessed is he who keeps the law.

30:11   There are those who curse their fathers and do not bless their mothers.

31:28   Her children rise up and call her blessed; her husband also, and he praises her.

Creation

8:22–31   The Lord possessed me at the beginning of his work, the first of his acts of old. Ages ago I was set up, at the first, before the beginning of the earth. When there were no depths I was brought forth, when there were no springs abounding with water. Before the mountains had been shaped, before the hills, I was brought forth, before he had made the earth with its fields, or the first of the dust of the world. When he established the heavens, I was there; when he drew a circle on the face of the deep, when he made firm the skies above, when he established the fountains of the deep, when he assigned to the sea its limit, so that the waters might not transgress his command, when he marked out the foundations of the earth, then I was beside him, like a master workman, and I was daily his delight, rejoicing before him always, rejoicing in his inhabited world and delighting in the children of man.

16:4   The Lord has made everything for its purpose, even the wicked for the day of trouble.

20:12   The hearing ear and the seeing eye, the Lord has made them both.

Evil Doers

1:10–19   My son, if sinners entice you, do not consent. If they say, "Come with us, let us lie in wait for blood; let us ambush the innocent without reason; like Sheol let us swallow them alive, and whole, like those who go down to the pit; we shall find all precious goods, we shall fill our houses with plunder; throw in your lot among us; we will all have one purse" – my son, do not walk in the way with them; hold back your foot from their paths, for their feet run to evil, and they make haste to shed blood. For in vain is a net spread in the sight of any bird, but these men lie in wait for their own blood; they set an ambush for their own lives. Such are the ways of everyone who is greedy for unjust gain; it takes away the life of its possessors.

2:12–15 Delivering you from the way of evil, from men of perverted speech, who forsake the paths of uprightness to walk in the ways of darkness, who rejoice in doing evil and delight in the perverseness of evil, men whose paths are crooked, and who are devious in their ways.

2:22 But the wicked will be cut off from the land, and the treacherous will be rooted out of it.

4:14–17 Do not enter the path of the wicked, and do not walk in the way of the evil. Avoid it; do not go on it; turn away from it and pass on. For they cannot sleep unless they have done wrong; they are robbed of sleep unless they have made someone stumble. For they eat the bread of wickedness and drink the wine of violence.

4:19 The way of the wicked is like deep darkness; they do not know over what they stumble.

5:21–23 For a man's ways are before the eyes of the Lord, and he ponders all his paths. The iniquities of the wicked ensnare him, and he is held fast in the cords of his sin. He dies for lack of discipline, and because of his great folly he is led astray.

6:12–15 A worthless person, a wicked man, goes about with crooked speech, winks with his eyes, signals with his feet, points with his finger, with perverted heart devises evil, continually sowing discord; therefore calamity will come upon him suddenly; in a moment he will be broken beyond healing.

8:13 The fear of the Lord is hatred of evil. Pride and arrogance and the way of evil and perverted speech I hate.

10:29 The way of the Lord is a stronghold to the blameless, but destruction to evildoers.

11:3 The integrity of the upright guides them, but the crookedness of the treacherous destroys them.

11:16–17 A gracious woman gets honor, and violent men get riches. A man who is kind benefits himself, but a cruel man hurts himself.

11:21   Be assured, an evil person will not go unpunished, but the offspring of the righteous will be delivered.

11:27   Whoever diligently seeks good seeks favor, but evil comes to him who searches for it.

12:2–3   A good man obtains favor from the Lord, but a man of evil devices he condemns. No one is established by wickedness, but the root of the righteous will never be moved.

12:20   Deceit is in the heart of those who devise evil, but those who plan peace have joy.

13:19   A desire fulfilled is sweet to the soul, but to turn away from evil is an abomination to fools.

14:17   A man of quick temper acts foolishly, and a man of evil devices is hated.

14:19   The evil bow down before the good, the wicked at the gates of the righteous.

14:22   Do they not go astray who devise evil? Those who devise good meet steadfast love and faithfulness.

15:3   The eyes of the Lord are in every place, keeping watch on the evil and the good.

15:26   The thoughts of the wicked are an abomination to the Lord, but gracious words are pure.

15:28   The heart of the righteous ponders how to answer, but the mouth of the wicked pours out evil things.

16:17   The highway of the upright turns aside from evil; whoever guards his way preserves his life.

16:27–29   A worthless man plots evil, and his speech is like a scorching fire. A dishonest man spreads strife, and a whisperer separates close friends. A man of violence entices his neighbor and leads him in a way that is not good.

17:4   An evildoer listens to wicked lips, and a liar gives ear to a mischievous tongue.

17:11   An evil man seeks only rebellion, and a cruel messenger will be sent against him.

17:13   If anyone returns evil for good, evil will not depart from his house.

17:20 A man of crooked heart does not discover good, and one with a dishonest tongue falls into calamity.

19:23 The fear of the Lord leads to life, and whoever has it rests satisfied; he will not be visited by harm.

20:22 Do not say, "I will repay evil"; wait for the Lord, and he will deliver you.

20:30 Blows that wound cleanse away evil; strokes make clean the innermost parts.

21:10 The soul of the wicked desires evil; his neighbor finds no mercy in his eyes.

22:5 Thorns and snares are in the way of the crooked; whoever guards his soul will keep far from them.

23:6–8 Do not eat the bread of a man who is stingy; do not desire his delicacies, for he is like one who is inwardly calculating. "Eat and drink!" he says to you, but his heart is not with you. You will vomit up the morsels that you have eaten, and waste your pleasant words.

24:1–2 Be not envious of evil men, nor desire to be with them, for their hearts devise violence, and their lips talk of trouble.

24:8–9 Whoever plans to do evil will be called a schemer. The devising of folly is sin, and the scoffer is an abomination to mankind.

24:19–20 Fret not yourself because of evildoers, and be not envious of the wicked, for the evil man has no future; the lamp of the wicked will be put out.

28:5 Evil men do not understand justice, but those who seek the Lord understand it completely.

28:10 Whoever misleads the upright into an evil way will fall into his own pit, but the blameless will have a goodly inheritance.

29:6 An evil man is ensnared in his transgression, but a righteous man sings and rejoices.

30:11–14 There are those who curse their fathers and do not bless their mothers. There are those who are clean in their own eyes but are not washed of their filth. There are those – how lofty are their eyes, how high their eyelids lift! There are those whose teeth are swords, whose fangs are knives, to devour the poor from off the earth, the needy from among mankind.

Fear of / Trust in the Lord

1:7 The fear of the Lord is the beginning of knowledge; fools despise wisdom and instruction.

1:28–31 Then they will call upon me, but I will not answer; they will seek me diligently but will not find me. Because they hated knowledge and did not choose the fear of the Lord, would have none of my counsel and despised all my reproof, therefore they shall eat the fruit of their way, and have their fill of their own devices.

2:1–5 My son, if you receive my words and treasure up my commandments with you, making your ear attentive to wisdom and inclining your heart to understanding; yes, if you call out for insight and raise your voice for understanding, if you seek it like silver and search for it as for hidden treasures, then you will understand the fear of the Lord and find the knowledge of God.

3:5–6 Trust in the Lord with all your heart, and do not lean on your own understanding. In all your ways acknowledge him, and he will make straight your paths.

3:7–8 Be not wise in your own eyes; fear the Lord, and turn away from evil. It will be healing to your flesh and refreshment to your bones.

8:13 The fear of the Lord is hatred of evil. Pride and arrogance and the way of evil and perverted speech I hate.

9:10–11 The fear of the Lord is the beginning of wisdom, and the knowledge of the Holy One is insight. For by me your days will be multiplied, and years will be added to your life.

10:27 The fear of the Lord prolongs life, but the years of the wicked will be short.

14:2 Whoever walks in uprightness fears the Lord, but he who is devious in his ways despises him.

14:26–27 In the fear of the Lord one has strong confidence, and his children will have a refuge. The fear of the Lord is a fountain of life, that one may turn away from the snares of death.

15:16   Better is a little with the fear of the Lord than great treasure and trouble with it.

15:33   The fear of the Lord is instruction in wisdom, and humility comes before honor.

16:6   By steadfast love and faithfulness iniquity is atoned for, and by the fear of the Lord one turns away from evil.

16:20   Whoever gives thought to the word will discover good, and blessed is he who trusts in the Lord.

19:23   The fear of the Lord leads to life, and whoever has it rests satisfied; he will not be visited by harm.

22:4   The reward for humility and fear of the Lord is riches and honor and life.

22:19   That your trust may be in the Lord, I have made them known to you today, even to you.

23:17–21   Let not your heart envy sinners, but continue in the fear of the Lord all the day. Surely there is a future, and your hope will not be cut off. Hear, my son, and be wise, and direct your heart in the way. Be not among drunkards or among gluttonous eaters of meat, for the drunkard and the glutton will come to poverty, and slumber will clothe them with rags.

24:21–22   My son, fear the Lord and the king, and do not join with those who do otherwise, for disaster from them will rise suddenly, and who knows the ruin that will come from them both?

28:14   Blessed is the one who fears the Lord always, but whoever hardens his heart will fall into calamity.

28:25   A greedy man stirs up strife, but the one who trusts in the Lord will be enriched.

29:25   The fear of man lays a snare, but whoever trusts in the Lord is safe.

31:30   Charm is deceitful, and beauty is vain, but a woman who fears the Lord is to be praised.

God's Delight

8:30   Then I was beside him, like a master workman, and I was daily his delight, rejoicing before him always.

11:1   A false balance is an abomination to the Lord, but a just weight is his delight.

11:20   Those of crooked heart are an abomination to the Lord, but those of blameless ways are his delight.

12:22   Lying lips are an abomination to the Lord, but those who act faithfully are his delight.

15:8   The sacrifice of the wicked is an abomination to the Lord, but the prayer of the upright is acceptable to him.

God/Lord

1:7   The fear of the Lord is the beginning of knowledge; fools despise wisdom and instruction.

1:29   Because they hated knowledge and did not choose the fear of the Lord.

2:5–8   Then you will understand the fear of the Lord and find the knowledge of God. For the Lord gives wisdom; from his mouth come knowledge and understanding; he stores up sound wisdom for the upright; he is a shield to those who walk in integrity, guarding the paths of justice and watching over the way of his saints.

2:16–17   So you will be delivered from the forbidden woman, from the adulteress with her smooth words, who forsakes the companion of her youth and forgets the covenant of her God.

3:4–10   So you will find favor and good success in the sight of God and man. Trust in the Lord with all your heart, and do not lean on your own understanding. In all your ways acknowledge him, and he will make straight your paths. Be not wise in your own eyes; fear the Lord, and turn away from evil. It will be healing to your flesh and refreshment to your bones. Honor the Lord with your wealth and with the firstfruits of all your produce; then your barns will be filled with plenty, and your vats will be bursting with wine.

3:11–12   My son, do not despise the Lord's discipline or be weary of his reproof, for the Lord reproves him whom he loves, as a father the son in whom he delights.

3:19–20   The Lord by wisdom founded the earth; by understanding he established the heavens; by his knowledge the deeps broke open, and the clouds drop down the dew.

3:26   For the Lord will be your confidence and will keep your foot from being caught.

3:32   For the devious person is an abomination to the Lord, but the upright are in his confidence.

3:33   The Lord's curse is on the house of the wicked, but he blesses the dwelling of the righteous.

5:21   For a man's ways are before the eyes of the Lord, and he ponders all his paths.

6:16–19   There are six things that the Lord hates, seven that are an abomination to him: haughty eyes, a lying tongue, and hands that shed innocent blood, a heart that devises wicked plans, feet that make haste to run to evil, a false witness who breathes out lies, and one who sows discord among brothers.

8:13   The fear of the Lord is hatred of evil. Pride and arrogance and the way of evil and perverted speech I hate.

8:22–31   The Lord possessed me at the beginning of his work, the first of his acts of old. Ages ago I was set up, at the first, before the beginning of the earth. When there were no depths I was brought forth, when there were no springs abounding with water. Before the mountains had been shaped, before the hills, I was brought forth, before he had made the earth with its fields, or the first of the dust of the world. When he established the heavens, I was there; when he drew a circle on the face of the deep, when he made firm the skies above, when he established the fountains of the deep, when he assigned to the sea its limit, so that the waters might not transgress his command, when he marked out the foundations of the earth, then I was beside him, like a master workman, and I was daily his delight, rejoicing before him always, rejoicing in his inhabited world and delighting in the children of man.

8:35   For whoever finds me finds life and obtains favor from the Lord.

9:10   The fear of the Lord is the beginning of wisdom, and the knowledge of the Holy One is insight.

10:3   The Lord does not let the righteous go hungry, but he thwarts the craving of the wicked.

10:22   The blessing of the Lord makes rich, and he adds no sorrow with it.

10:27   The fear of the Lord prolongs life, but the years of the wicked will be short.

10:29   The way of the Lord is a stronghold to the blameless, but destruction to evildoers.

11:1   A false balance is an abomination to the Lord, but a just weight is his delight.

11:20   Those of crooked heart are an abomination to the Lord, but those of blameless ways are his delight.

12:2   A good man obtains favor from the Lord, but a man of evil devices he condemns.

12:22   Lying lips are an abomination to the Lord, but those who act faithfully are his delight.

14:2   Whoever walks in uprightness fears the Lord, but he who is devious in his ways despises him.

14:26   In the fear of the Lord one has strong confidence, and his children will have a refuge.

14:27   The fear of the Lord is a fountain of life, that one may turn away from the snares of death.

14:31   Whoever oppresses a poor man insults his Maker, but he who is generous to the needy honors him.

15:3   The eyes of the Lord are in every place, keeping watch on the evil and the good.

15:8–9   The sacrifice of the wicked is an abomination to the Lord, but the prayer of the upright is acceptable to him. The way of the wicked is an abomination to the Lord, but he loves him who pursues righteousness.

15:11   Sheol and Abaddon lie open before the Lord; how much more the hearts of the children of man!

15:16   Better is a little with the fear of the Lord than great treasure and trouble with it.

15:25   The Lord tears down the house of the proud but maintains the widow's boundaries.

15:26   The thoughts of the wicked are an abomination to the Lord, but gracious words are pure.

15:29   The Lord is far from the wicked, but he hears the prayer of the righteous.

15:33   The fear of the Lord is instruction in wisdom, and humility comes before honor.

16:1–3   The plans of the heart belong to man, but the answer of the tongue is from the Lord. All the ways of a man are pure in his own eyes, but the Lord weighs the spirit. Commit your work to the Lord, and your plans will be established.

16:4   The Lord has made everything for its purpose, even the wicked for the day of trouble.

16:5   Everyone who is arrogant in heart is an abomination to the Lord; be assured, he will not go unpunished.

16:6   By steadfast love and faithfulness iniquity is atoned for, and by the fear of the Lord one turns away from evil.

16:7   When a man's ways please the Lord, he makes even his enemies to be at peace with him.

16:9   The heart of man plans his way, but the Lord establishes his steps.

16:11   A just balance and scales are the Lord's; all the weights in the bag are his work.

16:20   Whoever gives thought to the word will discover good, and blessed is he who trusts in the Lord.

16:33   The lot is cast into the lap, but its every decision is from the Lord.

17:3   The crucible is for silver, and the furnace is for gold, and the Lord tests hearts.

17:5   Whoever mocks the poor insults his Maker; he who is glad at calamity will not go unpunished.

17:15   He who justifies the wicked and he who condemns the righteous are both alike an abomination to the Lord.

18:10   The name of the Lord is a strong tower; the righteous man runs into it and is safe.

18:22   He who finds a wife finds a good thing and obtains favor from the Lord.

19:3   When a man's folly brings his way to ruin, his heart rages against the Lord.

19:14   House and wealth are inherited from fathers, but a prudent wife is from the Lord.

19:17   Whoever is generous to the poor lends to the Lord, and he will repay him for his deed.

19:21   Many are the plans in the mind of a man, but it is the purpose of the Lord that will stand.

19:23   The fear of the Lord leads to life, and whoever has it rests satisfied; he will not be visited by harm.

20:10   Unequal weights and unequal measures are both alike an abomination to the Lord.

20:12   The hearing ear and the seeing eye, the Lord has made them both.

20:22   Do not say, "I will repay evil"; wait for the Lord, and he will deliver you.

20:23   Unequal weights are an abomination to the Lord, and false scales are not good.

20:24   A man's steps are from the Lord; how then can man understand his way?

20:27   The spirit of man is the lamp of the Lord, searching all his innermost parts.

21:1–2   The king's heart is a stream of water in the hand of the Lord; he turns it wherever he will. Every way of a man is right in his own eyes, but the Lord weighs the heart.

21:3   To do righteousness and justice is more acceptable to the Lord than sacrifice.

21:12   The Righteous One observes the house of the wicked; he throws the wicked down to ruin.

21:30–31   No wisdom, no understanding, no counsel can avail against the Lord. The horse is made ready for the day of battle, but the victory belongs to the Lord.

22:2   The rich and the poor meet together; the Lord is the maker of them all.

22:4   The reward for humility and fear of the Lord is riches and honor and life.

22:12   The eyes of the Lord keep watch over knowledge, but he overthrows the words of the traitor.

22:14   The mouth of forbidden women is a deep pit; he with whom the Lord is angry will fall into it.

22:19   That your trust may be in the Lord, I have made them known to you today, even to you.

22:23   For the Lord will plead their cause and rob of life those who rob them.

23:10–12   Do not move an ancient landmark or enter the fields of the fatherless, for their Redeemer is strong; he will plead their cause against you. Apply your heart to instruction and your ear to words of knowledge.

23:17   Let not your heart envy sinners, but continue in the fear of the Lord all the day.

24:11–12   Rescue those who are being taken away to death; hold back those who are stumbling to the slaughter. If you say, "Behold, we did not know this," does not he who weighs the heart perceive it? Does not he who keeps watch over your soul know it, and will he not repay man according to his work?

24:17–18   Do not rejoice when your enemy falls, and let not your heart be glad when he stumbles, lest the Lord see it and be displeased, and turn away his anger from him.

25:2   It is the glory of God to conceal things, but the glory of kings is to search things out.

25:21–22   If your enemy is hungry, give him bread to eat, and if he is thirsty, give him water to drink, for you will heap burning coals on his head, and the Lord will reward you.

28:5   Evil men do not understand justice, but those who seek the Lord understand it completely.

28:25   A greedy man stirs up strife, but the one who trusts in the Lord will be enriched.

29:13   The poor man and the oppressor meet together; the Lord gives light to the eyes of both.

29:25   The fear of man lays a snare, but whoever trusts in the Lord is safe.

29:26   Many seek the face of a ruler, but it is from the Lord that a man gets justice.

30:5   Every word of God proves true; he is a shield to those who take refuge in him.

30:9   Lest I be full and deny you and say, "Who is the Lord?" or lest I be poor and steal and profane the name of my God.

31:30   Charm is deceitful, and beauty is vain, but a woman who fears the Lord is to be praised.

God's Word

13:13   Whoever despises the word brings destruction on himself, but he who reveres the commandment will be rewarded.

16:20   Whoever gives thought to the word will discover good, and blessed is he who trusts in the Lord.

19:16   Whoever keeps the commandment keeps his life; he who despises his ways will die.

30:5–6   Every word of God proves true; he is a shield to those who take refuge in him. Do not add to his words, lest he rebuke you and you be found a liar.

Good Man/Woman

2:20   So you will walk in the way of the good and keep to the paths of the righteous.

12:2   A good man obtains favor from the Lord, but a man of evil devices he condemns.

13:22 A good man leaves an inheritance to his children's children, but the sinner's wealth is laid up for the righteous.

14:14 The backslider in heart will be filled with the fruit of his ways, and a good man will be filled with the fruit of his ways.

14:22 Do they not go astray who devise evil? Those who devise good meet steadfast love and faithfulness.

15:3 The eyes of the Lord are in every place, keeping watch on the evil and the good.

19:17 Whoever is generous to the poor lends to the Lord, and he will repay him for his deed.

31:12 She does him good, and not harm, all the days of her life.

Life/Death

1:19 Such are the ways of everyone who is greedy for unjust gain; it takes away the life of its possessors.

2:18–19 For her house sinks down to death, and her paths to the departed; none who go to her come back, nor do they regain the paths of life.

3:2 For length of days and years of life and peace they will add to you.

3:16 Long life is in her right hand; in her left hand are riches and honor.

3:18 She is a tree of life to those who lay hold of her; those who hold her fast are called blessed.

3:22 And they will be life for your soul and adornment for your neck.

4:10 Hear, my son, and accept my words, that the years of your life may be many.

4:13 Keep hold of instruction; do not let go; guard her, for she is your life.

4:22–23 For they are life to those who find them, and healing to all their flesh. Keep your heart with all vigilance, for from it flow the springs of life.

5:5–6   Her feet go down to death; her steps follow the path to Sheol; she does not ponder the path of life; her ways wander, and she does not know it.

5:23   He dies for lack of discipline, and because of his great folly he is led astray.

6:23   For the commandment is a lamp and the teaching a light, and the reproofs of discipline are the way of life.

6:26   For the price of a prostitute is only a loaf of bread, but a married woman hunts down a precious life.

7:23   Till an arrow pierces its liver; as a bird rushes into a snare; he does not know that it will cost him his life.

7:27   Her house is the way to Sheol, going down to the chambers of death.

8:35–36   For whoever finds me finds life and obtains favor from the Lord, but he who fails to find me injures himself; all who hate me love death.

9:10–11   The fear of the Lord is the beginning of wisdom, and the knowledge of the Holy One is insight. For by me your days will be multiplied, and years will be added to your life.

9:13–18   The woman Folly is loud; she is seductive and knows nothing. She sits at the door of her house; she takes a seat on the highest places of the town, calling to those who pass by, who are going straight on their way, "Whoever is simple, let him turn in here!" And to him who lacks sense she says, "Stolen water is sweet, and bread eaten in secret is pleasant." But he does not know that the dead are there, that her guests are in the depths of Sheol.

10:2   Treasures gained by wickedness do not profit, but righteousness delivers from death.

10:11   The mouth of the righteous is a fountain of life, but the mouth of the wicked conceals violence.

10:16–17   The wage of the righteous leads to life, the gain of the wicked to sin. Whoever heeds instruction is on the path to life, but he who rejects reproof leads others astray.

10:21   The lips of the righteous feed many, but fools die for lack of sense.

10:27   The fear of the Lord prolongs life, but the years of the wicked will be short.

11:3   The integrity of the upright guides them, but the crookedness of the treacherous destroys them.

11:4   Riches do not profit in the day of wrath, but righteousness delivers from death.

11:19   Whoever is steadfast in righteousness will live, but he who pursues evil will die.

11:30   The fruit of the righteous is a tree of life, and whoever captures souls is wise.

12:10   Whoever is righteous has regard for the life of his beast, but the mercy of the wicked is cruel.

12:28   In the path of righteousness is life, and in its pathway there is no death.

13:3   Whoever guards his mouth preserves his life; he who opens wide his lips comes to ruin.

13:8   The ransom of a man's life is his wealth, but a poor man hears no threat.

13:12   Hope deferred makes the heart sick, but a desire fulfilled is a tree of life.

13:14   The teaching of the wise is a fountain of life, that one may turn away from the snares of death.

14:12   There is a way that seems right to a man, but its end is the way to death.

14:27   The fear of the Lord is a fountain of life, that one may turn away from the snares of death.

14:30   A tranquil heart gives life to the flesh, but envy makes the bones rot.

14:32   The wicked is overthrown through his evildoing, but the righteous finds refuge in his death.

15:4   A gentle tongue is a tree of life, but perverseness in it breaks the spirit.

15:10   There is severe discipline for him who forsakes the way; whoever hates reproof will die.

15:24   The path of life leads upward for the prudent, that he may turn away from Sheol beneath.

15:27   Whoever is greedy for unjust gain troubles his own household, but he who hates bribes will live.

16:14   A king's wrath is a messenger of death, and a wise man will appease it.

16:15   In the light of a king's face there is life, and his favor is like the clouds that bring the spring rain.

16:17   The highway of the upright turns aside from evil; whoever guards his way preserves his life.

16:22   Good sense is a fountain of life to him who has it, but the instruction of fools is folly.

16:25   There is a way that seems right to a man, but its end is the way to death.

18:21   Death and life are in the power of the tongue, and those who love it will eat its fruits.

19:16   Whoever keeps the commandment keeps his life; he who despises his ways will die.

19:18   Discipline your son, for there is hope; do not set your heart on putting him to death.

19:23   The fear of the Lord leads to life, and whoever has it rests satisfied; he will not be visited by harm.

20:2   The terror of a king is like the growling of a lion; whoever provokes him to anger forfeits his life.

21:6   The getting of treasures by a lying tongue is a fleeting vapor and a snare of death.

21:16   One who wanders from the way of good sense will rest in the assembly of the dead.

21:21   Whoever pursues righteousness and kindness will find life, righteousness, and honor.

21:25   The desire of the sluggard kills him, for his hands refuse to labor.

22:4   The reward for humility and fear of the Lord is riches and honor and life.

22:23   For the Lord will plead their cause and rob of life those who rob them.

23:13   Do not withhold discipline from a child; if you strike him with a rod, he will not die.

24:11–12   Rescue those who are being taken away to death; hold back those who are stumbling to the slaughter. If you say, "Behold, we did not know this," does not he who weighs the heart perceive it? Does not he who keeps watch over your soul know it, and will he not repay man according to his work?

26:18   Like a madman who throws firebrands, arrows, and death.

28:17   If one is burdened with the blood of another, he will be a fugitive until death; let no one help him.

29:10   Bloodthirsty men hate one who is blameless and seek the life of the upright.

29:24   The partner of a thief hates his own life; he hears the curse, but discloses nothing.

31:6   Give strong drink to the one who is perishing, and wine to those in bitter distress.

Prayer/Sacrifice

15:8   The sacrifice of the wicked is an abomination to the Lord, but the prayer of the upright is acceptable to him.

15:29   The Lord is far from the wicked, but he hears the prayer of the righteous.

20:25   It is a snare to say rashly, "It is holy," and to reflect only after making vows.

21:3   To do righteousness and justice is more acceptable to the Lord than sacrifice.

21:13   Whoever closes his ear to the cry of the poor will himself call out and not be answered.

21:27   The sacrifice of the wicked is an abomination; how much more when he brings it with evil intent.

28:9   If one turns away his ear from hearing the law, even his prayer is an abomination.

Reward

11:18   The wicked earns deceptive wages, but one who sows righteousness gets a sure reward.

11:31   If the righteous is repaid on earth, how much more the wicked and the sinner!

13:13   Whoever despises the word brings destruction on himself, but he who reveres the commandment will be rewarded.

13:21   Disaster pursues sinners, but the righteous are rewarded with good.

19:17   Whoever is generous to the poor lends to the Lord, and he will repay him for his deed.

22:4   The reward for humility and fear of the Lord is riches and honor and life.

25:21–22   If your enemy is hungry, give him bread to eat, and if he is thirsty, give him water to drink, for you will heap burning coals on his head, and the Lord will reward you.

Righteousness/Justice

1:3   To receive instruction in wise dealing, in righteousness, justice, and equity.

2:7–9   He stores up sound wisdom for the upright; he is a shield to those who walk in integrity, guarding the paths of justice and watching over the way of his saints. Then you will understand righteousness and justice and equity, every good path.

2:20–21   So you will walk in the way of the good and keep to the paths of the righteous. For the upright will inhabit the land, and those with integrity will remain in it.

3:32   For the devious person is an abomination to the Lord, but the upright are in his confidence.

4:11   I have taught you the way of wisdom; I have led you in the paths of uprightness.

4:18   But the path of the righteous is like the light of dawn, which shines brighter and brighter until full day.

4:25–27 Let your eyes look directly forward, and your gaze be straight before you. Ponder the path of your feet; then all your ways will be sure. Do not swerve to the right or to the left; turn your foot away from evil.

8:6 Hear, for I will speak noble things, and from my lips will come what is right.

8:8 All the words of my mouth are righteous; there is nothing twisted or crooked in them.

8:9 They are all straight to him who understands, and right to those who find knowledge.

8:15 By me kings reign, and rulers decree what is just.

8:18 Riches and honor are with me, enduring wealth and righteousness.

8:20–21 I walk in the way of righteousness, in the paths of justice, granting an inheritance to those who love me, and filling their treasuries.

10:2–3 Treasures gained by wickedness do not profit, but righteousness delivers from death. The Lord does not let the righteous go hungry, but he thwarts the craving of the wicked.

10:6–7 Blessings are on the head of the righteous, but the mouth of the wicked conceals violence. The memory of the righteous is a blessing, but the name of the wicked will rot.

10:11 The mouth of the righteous is a fountain of life, but the mouth of the wicked conceals violence.

10:16 The wage of the righteous leads to life, the gain of the wicked to sin.

10:20–21 The tongue of the righteous is choice silver; the heart of the wicked is of little worth. The lips of the righteous feed many, but fools die for lack of sense.

10:24–25 What the wicked dreads will come upon him, but the desire of the righteous will be granted. When the tempest passes, the wicked is no more, but the righteous is established forever.

10:28–32 The hope of the righteous brings joy, but the expectation of the wicked will perish. The way of the Lord is a stronghold to the blameless, but destruction to evildoers. The righteous will never be removed, but the wicked will not dwell in the land. The mouth of the righteous brings forth wisdom, but the perverse tongue will be cut off. The lips of the righteous know what is acceptable, but the mouth of the wicked, what is perverse.

11:3   The integrity of the upright guides them, but the crookedness of the treacherous destroys them.

11:4–6   Riches do not profit in the day of wrath, but righteousness delivers from death. The righteousness of the blameless keeps his way straight, but the wicked falls by his own wickedness. The righteousness of the upright delivers them, but the treacherous are taken captive by their lust.

11:8–11   The righteous is delivered from trouble, and the wicked walks into it instead. With his mouth the godless man would destroy his neighbor, but by knowledge the righteous are delivered. When it goes well with the righteous, the city rejoices, and when the wicked perish there are shouts of gladness. By the blessing of the upright a city is exalted, but by the mouth of the wicked it is overthrown.

11:18–19   The wicked earns deceptive wages, but one who sows righteousness gets a sure reward. Whoever is steadfast in righteousness will live, but he who pursues evil will die.

11:20   Those of crooked heart are an abomination to the Lord, but those of blameless ways are his delight.

11:21   Be assured, an evil person will not go unpunished, but the offspring of the righteous will be delivered.

11:23   The desire of the righteous ends only in good; the expectation of the wicked in wrath.

11:28   Whoever trusts in his riches will fall, but the righteous will flourish like a green leaf.

11:30–31   The fruit of the righteous is a tree of life, and whoever captures souls is wise. If the righteous is repaid on earth, how much more the wicked and the sinner!

12:3   No one is established by wickedness, but the root of the righteous will never be moved.

12:5–7   The thoughts of the righteous are just; the counsels of the wicked are deceitful. The words of the wicked lie in wait for blood, but the mouth of the upright delivers them. The wicked are overthrown and are no more, but the house of the righteous will stand.

12:10   Whoever is righteous has regard for the life of his beast, but the mercy of the wicked is cruel.

12:12–13   Whoever is wicked covets the spoil of evildoers, but the root of the righteous bears fruit. An evil man is ensnared by the transgression of his lips, but the righteous escapes from trouble.

12:21   No ill befalls the righteous, but the wicked are filled with trouble.

12:26   One who is righteous is a guide to his neighbor, but the way of the wicked leads them astray.

12:28   In the path of righteousness is life, and in its pathway there is no death.

13:5–6   The righteous hates falsehood, but the wicked brings shame and disgrace. Righteousness guards him whose way is blameless, but sin overthrows the wicked.

13:9   The light of the righteous rejoices, but the lamp of the wicked will be put out.

13:21   Disaster pursues sinners, but the righteous are rewarded with good.

13:23   The fallow ground of the poor would yield much food, but it is swept away through injustice.

13:25   The righteous has enough to satisfy his appetite, but the belly of the wicked suffers want.

14:2   Whoever walks in uprightness fears the Lord, but he who is devious in his ways despises him.

14:9   Fools mock at the guilt offering, but the upright enjoy acceptance.

14:11   The house of the wicked will be destroyed, but the tent of the upright will flourish.

14:19   The evil bow down before the good, the wicked at the gates of the righteous.

14:32   The wicked is overthrown through his evildoing, but the righteous finds refuge in his death.

14:34   Righteousness exalts a nation, but sin is a reproach to any people.

15:6   In the house of the righteous there is much treasure, but trouble befalls the income of the wicked.

15:8–9   The sacrifice of the wicked is an abomination to the Lord, but the prayer of the upright is acceptable to him. The way of the wicked is an abomination to the Lord, but he loves him who pursues righteousness.

15:19   The way of a sluggard is like a hedge of thorns, but the path of the upright is a level highway.

15:28–29   The heart of the righteous ponders how to answer, but the mouth of the wicked pours out evil things. The Lord is far from the wicked, but he hears the prayer of the righteous.

16:8   Better is a little with righteousness than great revenues with injustice.

16:12–13   It is an abomination to kings to do evil, for the throne is established by righteousness. Righteous lips are the delight of a king, and he loves him who speaks what is right.

16:17   The highway of the upright turns aside from evil; whoever guards his way preserves his life.

16:31   Gray hair is a crown of glory; it is gained in a righteous life.

17:26   To impose a fine on a righteous man is not good, nor to strike the noble for their uprightness.

18:5   It is not good to be partial to the wicked or to deprive the righteous of justice.

18:10   The name of the Lord is a strong tower; the righteous man runs into it and is safe.

20:7–8   The righteous who walks in his integrity – blessed are his children after him! A king who sits on the throne of judgment winnows all evil with his eyes.

20:11   Even a child makes himself known by his acts, by whether his conduct is pure and upright.

21:3   To do righteousness and justice is more acceptable to the Lord than sacrifice.

21:7–8   The violence of the wicked will sweep them away, because they refuse to do what is just. The way of the guilty is crooked, but the conduct of the pure is upright.

21:12   The Righteous One observes the house of the wicked; he throws the wicked down to ruin.

21:15   When justice is done, it is a joy to the righteous but terror to evildoers.

21:18   The wicked is a ransom for the righteous, and the traitor for the upright.

21:21   Whoever pursues righteousness and kindness will find life, righteousness, and honor.

21:26   All day long he craves and craves, but the righteous gives and does not hold back.

21:29   A wicked man puts on a bold face, but the upright gives thought to his ways.

23:16   My inmost being will exult when your lips speak what is right.

23:24–25   The father of the righteous will greatly rejoice; he who fathers a wise son will be glad in him. Let your father and mother be glad; let her who bore you rejoice.

24:15–16   Lie not in wait as a wicked man against the dwelling of the righteous; do no violence to his home; for the righteous falls seven times and rises again, but the wicked stumble in times of calamity.

24:23–26   These also are sayings of the wise. Partiality in judging is not good. Whoever says to the wicked, "You are in the right," will be cursed by peoples, abhorred by nations, but those who rebuke the wicked will have delight, and a good blessing will come upon them. Whoever gives an honest answer kisses the lips.

25:5   Take away the wicked from the presence of the king, and his throne will be established in righteousness.

25:26   Like a muddied spring or a polluted fountain is a righteous man who gives way before the wicked.

28:1   The wicked flee when no one pursues, but the righteous are bold as a lion.

28:5   Evil men do not understand justice, but those who seek the Lord understand it completely.

28:10   Whoever misleads the upright into an evil way will fall into his own pit, but the blameless will have a goodly inheritance.

28:12   When the righteous triumph, there is great glory, but when the wicked rise, people hide themselves.

28:28   When the wicked rise, people hide themselves, but when they perish, the righteous increase.

29:2   When the righteous increase, the people rejoice, but when the wicked rule, the people groan.

29:4   By justice a king builds up the land, but he who exacts gifts tears it down.

29:6–7   An evil man is ensnared in his transgression, but a righteous man sings and rejoices. A righteous man knows the rights of the poor; a wicked man does not understand such knowledge.

29:10   Bloodthirsty men hate one who is blameless and seek the life of the upright.

29:16   When the wicked increase, transgression increases, but the righteous will look upon their downfall.

29:26   Many seek the face of a ruler, but it is from the Lord that a man gets justice.

29:27   An unjust man is an abomination to the righteous, but one whose way is straight is an abomination to the wicked.

31:8–9   Open your mouth for the mute, for the rights of all who are destitute. Open your mouth, judge righteously, defend the rights of the poor and needy.

Sin

5:22   The iniquities of the wicked ensnare him, and he is held fast in the cords of his sin.

14:9   Fools mock at the guilt offering, but the upright enjoy acceptance.

14:34   Righteousness exalts a nation, but sin is a reproach to any people.

16:6   By steadfast love and faithfulness iniquity is atoned for, and by the fear of the Lord one turns away from evil.

17:19   Whoever loves transgression loves strife; he who makes his door high seeks destruction.

19:28   A worthless witness mocks at justice, and the mouth of the wicked devours iniquity.

20:9   Who can say, "I have made my heart pure; I am clean from my sin"?

21:4   Haughty eyes and a proud heart, the lamp of the wicked, are sin.

21:8   The way of the guilty is crooked, but the conduct of the pure is upright.

21:15   When justice is done, it is a joy to the righteous but terror to evildoers.

22:8   Whoever sows injustice will reap calamity, and the rod of his fury will fail.

24:8–9   Whoever plans to do evil will be called a schemer. The devising of folly is sin, and the scoffer is an abomination to mankind.

28:13   Whoever conceals his transgressions will not prosper, but he who confesses and forsakes them will obtain mercy.

28:17   If one is burdened with the blood of another, he will be a fugitive until death; let no one help him.

29:6   An evil man is ensnared in his transgression, but a righteous man sings and rejoices.

29:16   When the wicked increase, transgression increases, but the righteous will look upon their downfall.

29:22   A man of wrath stirs up strife, and one given to anger causes much transgression.

Way/Will of the Lord

10:29   The way of the Lord is a stronghold to the blameless, but destruction to evildoers.

16:20   Whoever gives thought to the word will discover good, and blessed is he who trusts in the Lord.

Wickedness

1:10   My son, if sinners entice you, do not consent.

2:22   But the wicked will be cut off from the land, and the treacherous will be rooted out of it.

3:25   Do not be afraid of sudden terror or of the ruin of the wicked, when it comes.

3:33   The Lord's curse is on the house of the wicked, but he blesses the dwelling of the righteous.

4:14   Do not enter the path of the wicked, and do not walk in the way of the evil.

4:17   For they eat the bread of wickedness and drink the wine of violence.

4:19   The way of the wicked is like deep darkness; they do not know over what they stumble.

5:22   The iniquities of the wicked ensnare him, and he is held fast in the cords of his sin.

6:12   A worthless person, a wicked man, goes about with crooked speech.

6:18   A heart that devises wicked plans, feet that make haste to run to evil...

8:7   For my mouth will utter truth; wickedness is an abomination to my lips.

8:36   But he who fails to find me injures himself; all who hate me love death.

9:7   Whoever corrects a scoffer gets himself abuse, and he who reproves a wicked man incurs injury.

10:3   The Lord does not let the righteous go hungry, but he thwarts the craving of the wicked.

10:6–7   Blessings are on the head of the righteous, but the mouth of the wicked conceals violence. The memory of the righteous is a blessing, but the name of the wicked will rot.

10:11   The mouth of the righteous is a fountain of life, but the mouth of the wicked conceals violence.

10:16   The wage of the righteous leads to life, the gain of the wicked to sin.

10:20   The tongue of the righteous is choice silver; the heart of the wicked is of little worth.

10:23–25   Doing wrong is like a joke to a fool, but wisdom is pleasure to a man of understanding. What the wicked dreads will come upon him, but the desire of the righteous will be granted. When the tempest passes, the wicked is no more, but the righteous is established forever.

10:27–32   The fear of the Lord prolongs life, but the years of the wicked will be short. The hope of the righteous brings joy, but the expectation of the wicked will perish. The way of the Lord is a stronghold to the blameless, but destruction to evildoers. The righteous will never be removed, but the wicked will not dwell in the land. The mouth of the righteous brings forth wisdom, but the perverse tongue will be cut off. The lips of the righteous know what is acceptable, but the mouth of the wicked, what is perverse.

11:5–11   The righteousness of the blameless keeps his way straight, but the wicked falls by his own wickedness. The righteousness of the upright delivers them, but the treacherous are taken captive by their lust. When the wicked dies, his hope will perish, and the expectation of wealth perishes too. The righteous is delivered from trouble, and the wicked walks into it instead. With his mouth the godless man would destroy his neighbor, but by knowledge the righteous are delivered. When it goes well with the righteous, the city rejoices, and when the wicked perish there are shouts of gladness. By the blessing of the upright a city is exalted, but by the mouth of the wicked it is overthrown.

11:18–19   The wicked earns deceptive wages, but one who sows righteousness gets a sure reward. Whoever is steadfast in righteousness will live, but he who pursues evil will die.

11:23   The desire of the righteous ends only in good; the expectation of the wicked in wrath.

11:31   If the righteous is repaid on earth, how much more the wicked and the sinner!

12:3   No one is established by wickedness, but the root of the righteous will never be moved.

12:5–7   The thoughts of the righteous are just; the counsels of the wicked are deceitful. The words of the wicked lie in wait for blood, but the mouth of the upright delivers them. The wicked are overthrown and are no more, but the house of the righteous will stand.

12:10   Whoever is righteous has regard for the life of his beast, but the mercy of the wicked is cruel.

12:12–13   Whoever is wicked covets the spoil of evildoers, but the root of the righteous bears fruit. An evil man is ensnared by the transgression of his lips, but the righteous escapes from trouble.

12:21   No ill befalls the righteous, but the wicked are filled with trouble.

12:26   One who is righteous is a guide to his neighbor, but the way of the wicked leads them astray.

13:5–6   The righteous hates falsehood, but the wicked brings shame and disgrace. Righteousness guards him whose way is blameless, but sin overthrows the wicked.

13:9   The light of the righteous rejoices, but the lamp of the wicked will be put out.

13:17   A wicked messenger falls into trouble, but a faithful envoy brings healing.

13:21–22   Disaster pursues sinners, but the righteous are rewarded with good. A good man leaves an inheritance to his children's children, but the sinner's wealth is laid up for the righteous.

13:25   The righteous has enough to satisfy his appetite, but the belly of the wicked suffers want.

14:9   Fools mock at the guilt offering, but the upright enjoy acceptance.

14:11   The house of the wicked will be destroyed, but the tent of the upright will flourish.

14:14   The backslider in heart will be filled with the fruit of his ways, and a good man will be filled with the fruit of his ways.

14:19   The evil bow down before the good, the wicked at the gates of the righteous.

14:21   Whoever despises his neighbor is a sinner, but blessed is he who is generous to the poor.

14:32   The wicked is overthrown through his evildoing, but the righteous finds refuge in his death.

14:34   Righteousness exalts a nation, but sin is a reproach to any people.

15:6   In the house of the righteous there is much treasure, but trouble befalls the income of the wicked.

15:8–9   The sacrifice of the wicked is an abomination to the Lord, but the prayer of the upright is acceptable to him. The way of the wicked is an abomination to the Lord, but he loves him who pursues righteousness.

15:28–29   The heart of the righteous ponders how to answer, but the mouth of the wicked pours out evil things. The Lord is far from the wicked, but he hears the prayer of the righteous.

16:4   The Lord has made everything for its purpose, even the wicked for the day of trouble.

16:12   It is an abomination to kings to do evil, for the throne is established by righteousness.

17:4   An evildoer listens to wicked lips, and a liar gives ear to a mischievous tongue.

17:15   He who justifies the wicked and he who condemns the righteous are both alike an abomination to the Lord.

17:23   The wicked accepts a bribe in secret to pervert the ways of justice.

18:3   When wickedness comes, contempt comes also, and with dishonor comes disgrace.

18:5   It is not good to be partial to the wicked or to deprive the righteous of justice.

19:28   A worthless witness mocks at justice, and the mouth of the wicked devours iniquity.

20:9   Who can say, "I have made my heart pure; I am clean from my sin"?

20:26   A wise king winnows the wicked and drives the wheel over them.

21:4   Haughty eyes and a proud heart, the lamp of the wicked, are sin.

21:7   The violence of the wicked will sweep them away, because they refuse to do what is just.

21:10   The soul of the wicked desires evil; his neighbor finds no mercy in his eyes.

21:12   The Righteous One observes the house of the wicked; he throws the wicked down to ruin.

21:18   The wicked is a ransom for the righteous, and the traitor for the upright.

21:27   The sacrifice of the wicked is an abomination; how much more when he brings it with evil intent.

21:29   A wicked man puts on a bold face, but the upright gives thought to his ways.

23:17   Let not your heart envy sinners, but continue in the fear of the Lord all the day.

24:9   The devising of folly is sin, and the scoffer is an abomination to mankind.

24:15–16   Lie not in wait as a wicked man against the dwelling of the righteous; do no violence to his home; for the righteous falls seven times and rises again, but the wicked stumble in times of calamity.

24:19–20   Fret not yourself because of evildoers, and be not envious of the wicked, for the evil man has no future; the lamp of the wicked will be put out.

24:23–26   These also are sayings of the wise. Partiality in judging is not good. Whoever says to the wicked, "You are in the right," will be cursed by peoples, abhorred by nations, but those who rebuke the wicked will have delight, and a good blessing will come upon them. Whoever gives an honest answer kisses the lips.

25:5 Take away the wicked from the presence of the king, and his throne will be established in righteousness.

25:26 Like a muddied spring or a polluted fountain is a righteous man who gives way before the wicked.

26:23 Like the glaze covering an earthen vessel are fervent lips with an evil heart.

26:26 Though his hatred be covered with deception, his wickedness will be exposed in the assembly.

28:1 The wicked flee when no one pursues, but the righteous are bold as a lion.

28:4 Those who forsake the law praise the wicked, but those who keep the law strive against them.

28:12 When the righteous triumph, there is great glory, but when the wicked rise, people hide themselves.

28:15 Like a roaring lion or a charging bear is a wicked ruler over a poor people.

28:28 When the wicked rise, people hide themselves, but when they perish, the righteous increase.

29:2 When the righteous increase, the people rejoice, but when the wicked rule, the people groan.

29:7 A righteous man knows the rights of the poor; a wicked man does not understand such knowledge.

29:12 If a ruler listens to falsehood, all his officials will be wicked.

29:16 When the wicked increase, transgression increases, but the righteous will look upon their downfall.

29:27 An unjust man is an abomination to the righteous, but one whose way is straight is an abomination to the wicked.

30:21–23 Under three things the earth trembles; under four it cannot bear up: a slave when he becomes king, and a fool when he is filled with food; an unloved woman when she gets a husband, and a maidservant when she displaces her mistress.

7

PERSONAL WISDOM

Alcohol

4:17 For they eat the bread of wickedness and drink the wine of violence.

20:1 Wine is a mocker, strong drink a brawler, and whoever is led astray by it is not wise.

21:17 Whoever loves pleasure will be a poor man; he who loves wine and oil will not be rich.

23:19–21 Hear, my son, and be wise, and direct your heart in the way. Be not among drunkards or among gluttonous eaters of meat, for the drunkard and the glutton will come to poverty, and slumber will clothe them with rags.

23:29–35 Who has woe? Who has sorrow? Who has strife? Who has complaining? Who has wounds without cause? Who has redness of eyes? Those who tarry long over wine; those who go to try mixed wine. Do not look at wine when it is red, when it sparkles in the cup and goes down smoothly. In the end it bites like a serpent and stings like an adder. Your eyes will see strange things, and your heart utter perverse things. You will be like one who lies down in the midst of the sea, like one who lies on the top of a mast. "They struck me," you will say, "but I was not hurt; they beat me, but I did not feel it. When shall I awake? I must have another drink."

26:9   Like a thorn that goes up into the hand of a drunkard is a proverb in the mouth of fools.

31:4–7   It is not for kings, O Lemuel, it is not for kings to drink wine, or for rulers to take strong drink, lest they drink and forget what has been decreed and pervert the rights of all the afflicted. Give strong drink to the one who is perishing, and wine to those in bitter distress; let them drink and forget their poverty and remember their misery no more.

Anger/Violence/Wrath

1:19   Such are the ways of everyone who is greedy for unjust gain; it takes away the life of its possessors.

3:31–35   Do not envy a man of violence and do not choose any of his ways, for the devious person is an abomination to the Lord, but the upright are in his confidence. The Lord's curse is on the house of the wicked, but he blesses the dwelling of the righteous. Toward the scorners he is scornful, but to the humble he gives favor. The wise will inherit honor, but fools get disgrace.

4:17   For they eat the bread of wickedness and drink the wine of violence.

6:14   With perverted heart devises evil, continually sowing discord.

6:17   Haughty eyes, a lying tongue, and hands that shed innocent blood.

6:19   A false witness who breathes out lies, and one who sows discord among brothers.

6:34   For jealousy makes a man furious, and he will not spare when he takes revenge.

10:6   Blessings are on the head of the righteous, but the mouth of the wicked conceals violence.

10:11   The mouth of the righteous is a fountain of life, but the mouth of the wicked conceals violence.

10:12   Hatred stirs up strife, but love covers all offenses.

11:4   Riches do not profit in the day of wrath, but righteousness delivers from death.

11:23   The desire of the righteous ends only in good; the expectation of the wicked in wrath.

13:2   From the fruit of his mouth a man eats what is good, but the desire of the treacherous is for violence.

13:10   By insolence comes nothing but strife, but with those who take advice is wisdom.

14:17   A man of quick temper acts foolishly, and a man of evil devices is hated.

14:29   Whoever is slow to anger has great understanding, but he who has a hasty temper exalts folly.

14:35   A servant who deals wisely has the king's favor, but his wrath falls on one who acts shamefully.

15:1   A soft answer turns away wrath, but a harsh word stirs up anger.

15:18   A hot–tempered man stirs up strife, but he who is slow to anger quiets contention.

16:14   A king's wrath is a messenger of death, and a wise man will appease it.

16:28   A dishonest man spreads strife, and a whisperer separates close friends.

16:29   A man of violence entices his neighbor and leads him in a way that is not good.

16:32   Whoever is slow to anger is better than the mighty, and he who rules his spirit than he who takes a city.

17:1   Better is a dry morsel with quiet than a house full of feasting with strife.

17:14   The beginning of strife is like letting out water, so quit before the quarrel breaks out.

17:19   Whoever loves transgression loves strife; he who makes his door high seeks destruction.

17:27   Whoever restrains his words has knowledge, and he who has a cool spirit is a man of understanding.

18:6   A fool's lips walk into a fight, and his mouth invites a beating.

18:19　A brother offended is more unyielding than a strong city, and quarreling is like the bars of a castle.

19:11　Good sense makes one slow to anger, and it is his glory to overlook an offense.

19:12　A king's wrath is like the growling of a lion, but his favor is like dew on the grass.

19:19　A man of great wrath will pay the penalty, for if you deliver him, you will only have to do it again.

20:2　The terror of a king is like the growling of a lion; whoever provokes him to anger forfeits his life.

20:3　It is an honor for a man to keep aloof from strife, but every fool will be quarreling.

21:7　The violence of the wicked will sweep them away, because they refuse to do what is just.

21:14　A gift in secret averts anger, and a concealed bribe, strong wrath.

22:8　Whoever sows injustice will reap calamity, and the rod of his fury will fail.

22:10　Drive out a scoffer, and strife will go out, and quarreling and abuse will cease.

22:24–25　Make no friendship with a man given to anger, nor go with a wrathful man, lest you learn his ways and entangle yourself in a snare.

24:2　For their hearts devise violence, and their lips talk of trouble.

25:23　The north wind brings forth rain, and a backbiting tongue, angry looks.

25:28　A man without self-control is like a city broken into and left without walls.

26:6　Whoever sends a message by the hand of a fool cuts off his own feet and drinks violence.

26:17　Whoever meddles in a quarrel not his own is like one who takes a passing dog by the ears.

26:21　As charcoal to hot embers and wood to fire, so is a quarrelsome man for kindling strife.

27:3   A stone is heavy, and sand is weighty, but a fool's provocation is heavier than both.

27:4   Wrath is cruel, anger is overwhelming, but who can stand before jealousy?

28:17   If one is burdened with the blood of another, he will be a fugitive until death; let no one help him.

28:25   A greedy man stirs up strife, but the one who trusts in the Lord will be enriched.

29:8   Scoffers set a city aflame, but the wise turn away wrath.

29:9   If a wise man has an argument with a fool, the fool only rages and laughs, and there is no quiet.

29:11   A fool gives full vent to his spirit, but a wise man quietly holds it back.

29:22   A man of wrath stirs up strife, and one given to anger causes much transgression.

30:32–33   If you have been foolish, exalting yourself, or if you have been devising evil, put your hand on your mouth. For pressing milk produces curds, pressing the nose produces blood, and pressing anger produces strife.

Counsel

1:5   Let the wise hear and increase in learning, and the one who understands obtain guidance.

1:25   Because you have ignored all my counsel and would have none of my reproof.

1:30   Would have none of my counsel and despised all my reproof.

6:22   When you walk, they will lead you; when you lie down, they will watch over you; and when you awake, they will talk with you.

8:14   I have counsel and sound wisdom; I have insight; I have strength.

11:3   The integrity of the upright guides them, but the crookedness of the treacherous destroys them.

11:14   Where there is no guidance, a people falls, but in an abundance of counselors there is safety.

12:5   The thoughts of the righteous are just; the counsels of the wicked are deceitful.

12:15   The way of a fool is right in his own eyes, but a wise man listens to advice.

12:20   Deceit is in the heart of those who devise evil, but those who plan peace have joy.

12:26   One who is righteous is a guide to his neighbor, but the way of the wicked leads them astray.

13:10   By insolence comes nothing but strife, but with those who take advice is wisdom.

15:22   Without counsel plans fail, but with many advisers they succeed.

18:1   Whoever isolates himself seeks his own desire; he breaks out against all sound judgment.

19:20–21   Listen to advice and accept instruction, that you may gain wisdom in the future. Many are the plans in the mind of a man, but it is the purpose of the Lord that will stand.

20:18   Plans are established by counsel; by wise guidance wage war.

21:30   No wisdom, no understanding, no counsel can avail against the Lord.

22:20–21   Have I not written for you thirty sayings of counsel and knowledge, to make you know what is right and true, that you may give a true answer to those who sent you?

24:3–6   By wisdom a house is built, and by understanding it is established; by knowledge the rooms are filled with all precious and pleasant riches. A wise man is full of strength, and a man of knowledge enhances his might, for by wise guidance you can wage your war, and in abundance of counselors there is victory.

27:9   Oil and perfume make the heart glad, and the sweetness of a friend comes from his earnest counsel.

Foolishness

1:7 The fear of the Lord is the beginning of knowledge; fools despise wisdom and instruction.

1:20–33 Wisdom cries aloud in the street, in the markets she raises her voice; at the head of the noisy streets she cries out; at the entrance of the city gates she speaks: How long, O simple ones, will you love being simple? How long will scoffers delight in their scoffing and fools hate knowledge? If you turn at my reproof, behold, I will pour out my spirit to you; I will make my words known to you. Because I have called and you refused to listen, have stretched out my hand and no one has heeded, because you have ignored all my counsel and would have none of my reproof, I also will laugh at your calamity; I will mock when terror strikes you, when terror strikes you like a storm and your calamity comes like a whirlwind, when distress and anguish come upon you. Then they will call upon me, but I will not answer; they will seek me diligently but will not find me. Because they hated knowledge and did not choose the fear of the Lord, would have none of my counsel and despised all my reproof, therefore they shall eat the fruit of their way, and have their fill of their own devices. For the simple are killed by their turning away, and the complacency of fools destroys them; but whoever listens to me will dwell secure and will be at ease, without dread of disaster.

3:34–35 Toward the scorners he is scornful, but to the humble he gives favor. The wise will inherit honor, but fools get disgrace.

5:23 He dies for lack of discipline, and because of his great folly he is led astray.

7:22 All at once he follows her, as an ox goes to the slaughter, or as a stag is caught fast.

8:5 O simple ones, learn prudence; O fools, learn sense.

9:6 Leave your simple ways, and live, and walk in the way of insight.

9:7 Whoever corrects a scoffer gets himself abuse, and he who reproves a wicked man incurs injury.

9:8 Do not reprove a scoffer, or he will hate you; reprove a wise man, and he will love you.

9:13–18   The woman Folly is loud; she is seductive and knows nothing. She sits at the door of her house; she takes a seat on the highest places of the town, calling to those who pass by, who are going straight on their way, "Whoever is simple, let him turn in here!" And to him who lacks sense she says, "Stolen water is sweet, and bread eaten in secret is pleasant." But he does not know that the dead are there, that her guests are in the depths of Sheol.

10:1   The proverbs of Solomon. A wise son makes a glad father, but a foolish son is a sorrow to his mother.

10:8   The wise of heart will receive commandments, but a babbling fool will come to ruin.

10:10   Whoever winks the eye causes trouble, but a babbling fool will come to ruin.

10:14   The wise lay up knowledge, but the mouth of a fool brings ruin near.

10:18   The one who conceals hatred has lying lips, and whoever utters slander is a fool.

10:21   The lips of the righteous feed many, but fools die for lack of sense.

10:23   Doing wrong is like a joke to a fool, but wisdom is pleasure to a man of understanding.

11:29   Whoever troubles his own household will inherit the wind, and the fool will be servant to the wise of heart.

12:15–16   The way of a fool is right in his own eyes, but a wise man listens to advice. The vexation of a fool is known at once, but the prudent ignores an insult.

12:23   A prudent man conceals knowledge, but the heart of fools proclaims folly.

13:1   A wise son hears his father's instruction, but a scoffer does not listen to rebuke.

13:16   In everything the prudent acts with knowledge, but a fool flaunts his folly.

13:19–20   A desire fulfilled is sweet to the soul, but to turn away from evil is an abomination to fools. Whoever walks with the wise becomes wise, but the companion of fools will suffer harm.

14:1   The wisest of women builds her house, but folly with her own hands tears it down.

14:3   By the mouth of a fool comes a rod for his back, but the lips of the wise will preserve them.

14:6   A scoffer seeks wisdom in vain, but knowledge is easy for a man of understanding.

14:7–9   Leave the presence of a fool, for there you do not meet words of knowledge. The wisdom of the prudent is to discern his way, but the folly of fools is deceiving. Fools mock at the guilt offering, but the upright enjoy acceptance.

14:16   One who is wise is cautious and turns away from evil, but a fool is reckless and careless.

14:18   The simple inherit folly, but the prudent are crowned with knowledge.

14:24   The crown of the wise is their wealth, but the folly of fools brings folly.

14:29   Whoever is slow to anger has great understanding, but he who has a hasty temper exalts folly.

14:33   Wisdom rests in the heart of a man of understanding, but it makes itself known even in the midst of fools.

14:35   A servant who deals wisely has the king's favor, but his wrath falls on one who acts shamefully.

15:2   The tongue of the wise commends knowledge, but the mouths of fools pour out folly.

15:5   A fool despises his father's instruction, but whoever heeds reproof is prudent.

15:7   The lips of the wise spread knowledge; not so the hearts of fools.

15:12   A scoffer does not like to be reproved; he will not go to the wise.

15:14   The heart of him who has understanding seeks knowledge, but the mouths of fools feed on folly.

15:20–21   A wise son makes a glad father, but a foolish man despises his mother. Folly is a joy to him who lacks sense, but a man of understanding walks straight ahead.

16:22   Good sense is a fountain of life to him who has it, but the instruction of fools is folly.

17:7   Fine speech is not becoming to a fool; still less is false speech to a prince.

17:10   A rebuke goes deeper into a man of understanding than a hundred blows into a fool.

17:12   Let a man meet a she-bear robbed of her cubs rather than a fool in his folly.

17:16   Why should a fool have money in his hand to buy wisdom when he has no sense?

17:21   He who sires a fool gets himself sorrow, and the father of a fool has no joy.

17:24–25   The discerning sets his face toward wisdom, but the eyes of a fool are on the ends of the earth. A foolish son is a grief to his father and bitterness to her who bore him.

17:28   Even a fool who keeps silent is considered wise; when he closes his lips, he is deemed intelligent.

18:2   A fool takes no pleasure in understanding, but only in expressing his opinion.

18:5   It is not good to be partial to the wicked or to deprive the righteous of justice.

18:6–7   A fool's lips walk into a fight, and his mouth invites a beating. A fool's mouth is his ruin, and his lips are a snare to his soul.

18:13   If one gives an answer before he hears, it is his folly and shame.

19:1   Better is a poor person who walks in his integrity than one who is crooked in speech and is a fool.

19:3   When a man's folly brings his way to ruin, his heart rages against the Lord.

19:10   It is not fitting for a fool to live in luxury, much less for a slave to rule over princes.

19:13   A foolish son is ruin to his father, and a wife's quarreling is a continual dripping of rain.

19:25   Strike a scoffer, and the simple will learn prudence; reprove a man of understanding, and he will gain knowledge.

19:29   Condemnation is ready for scoffers, and beating for the backs of fools.

20:1   Wine is a mocker, strong drink a brawler, and whoever is led astray by it is not wise.

20:3   It is an honor for a man to keep aloof from strife, but every fool will be quarreling.

21:11   When a scoffer is punished, the simple becomes wise; when a wise man is instructed, he gains knowledge.

21:20   Precious treasure and oil are in a wise man's dwelling, but a foolish man devours it.

21:24   "Scoffer" is the name of the arrogant, haughty man who acts with arrogant pride.

22:3   The prudent sees danger and hides himself, but the simple go on and suffer for it.

22:10   Drive out a scoffer, and strife will go out, and quarreling and abuse will cease.

22:15   Folly is bound up in the heart of a child, but the rod of discipline drives it far from him.

23:9   Do not speak in the hearing of a fool, for he will despise the good sense of your words.

24:7   Wisdom is too high for a fool; in the gate he does not open his mouth.

24:9   The devising of folly is sin, and the scoffer is an abomination to mankind.

25:19   Trusting in a treacherous man in time of trouble is like a bad tooth or a foot that slips.

26:1–12   Like snow in summer or rain in harvest, so honor is not fitting for a fool. Like a sparrow in its flitting, like a swallow in its flying, a curse that is causeless does not alight. A whip for the horse, a bridle for the donkey, and a rod for the back of fools. Answer not a fool according to his folly, lest you be like him yourself. Answer a fool according to his folly, lest he be wise in his own eyes. Whoever sends a message by the hand of a fool cuts off his own feet and drinks violence. Like a lame man's legs, which hang useless, is a proverb in the mouth of fools. Like one who binds the stone in the sling is one who gives honor to a fool. Like a thorn that goes up into the hand of a drunkard is a proverb in the mouth of fools. Like an archer who wounds everybody is one who hires a passing fool or drunkard. Like a dog that returns to his vomit is a fool who repeats his folly. Do you see a man who is wise in his own eyes? There is more hope for a fool than for him.

27:3   A stone is heavy, and sand is weighty, but a fool's provocation is heavier than both.

27:12   The prudent sees danger and hides himself, but the simple go on and suffer for it.

27:22   Crush a fool in a mortar with a pestle along with crushed grain, yet his folly will not depart from him.

28:26   Whoever trusts in his own mind is a fool, but he who walks in wisdom will be delivered.

29:8–9   Scoffers set a city aflame, but the wise turn away wrath. If a wise man has an argument with a fool, the fool only rages and laughs, and there is no quiet.

29:11   A fool gives full vent to his spirit, but a wise man quietly holds it back.

29:20   Do you see a man who is hasty in his words? There is more hope for a fool than for him.

30:22   A slave when he becomes king, and a fool when he is filled with food.

30:32   If you have been foolish, exalting yourself, or if you have been devising evil, put your hand on your mouth.

Greed

11:6   The righteousness of the upright delivers them, but the treacherous are taken captive by their lust.

11:26   The people curse him who holds back grain, but a blessing is on the head of him who sells it.

23:20–21   Be not among drunkards or among gluttonous eaters of meat, for the drunkard and the glutton will come to poverty, and slumber will clothe them with rags.

25:16   If you have found honey, eat only enough for you, lest you have your fill of it and vomit it.

27:7   One who is full loathes honey, but to one who is hungry everything bitter is sweet.

27:20   Sheol and Abaddon are never satisfied, and never satisfied are the eyes of man.

28:7   The one who keeps the law is a son with understanding, but a companion of gluttons shames his father.

30:15–16   The leech has two daughters; "Give" and "Give," they cry. Three things are never satisfied; four never say, "Enough": Sheol, the barren womb, the land never satisfied with water, and the fire that never says, "Enough."

Health/Peace/Wellbeing

3:2   For length of days and years of life and peace they will add to you.

3:7–8   Be not wise in your own eyes; fear the Lord, and turn away from evil. It will be healing to your flesh and refreshment to your bones.

3:17–18   Her ways are ways of pleasantness, and all her paths are peace. She is a tree of life to those who lay hold of her; those who hold her fast are called blessed.

4:20–22   My son, be attentive to my words; incline your ear to my sayings. Let them not escape from your sight; keep them within your heart. For they are life to those who find them, and healing to all their flesh.

6:15   Therefore calamity will come upon him suddenly; in a moment he will be broken beyond healing.

10:1   The proverbs of Solomon. A wise son makes a glad father, but a foolish son is a sorrow to his mother.

11:10   When it goes well with the righteous, the city rejoices, and when the wicked perish there are shouts of gladness.

11:30   The fruit of the righteous is a tree of life, and whoever captures souls is wise.

12:18   There is one whose rash words are like sword thrusts, but the tongue of the wise brings healing.

12:20   Deceit is in the heart of those who devise evil, but those who plan peace have joy.

12:25   Anxiety in a man's heart weighs him down, but a good word makes him glad.

13:12   Hope deferred makes the heart sick, but a desire fulfilled is a tree of life.

13:17   A wicked messenger falls into trouble, but a faithful envoy brings healing.

13:19   A desire fulfilled is sweet to the soul, but to turn away from evil is an abomination to fools.

14:10   The heart knows its own bitterness, and no stranger shares its joy.

14:13   Even in laughter the heart may ache, and the end of joy may be grief.

14:30   A tranquil heart gives life to the flesh, but envy makes the bones rot.

15:4   A gentle tongue is a tree of life, but perverseness in it breaks the spirit.

15:13   A glad heart makes a cheerful face, but by sorrow of heart the spirit is crushed.

15:15   All the days of the afflicted are evil, but the cheerful of heart has a continual feast.

15:20–21   A wise son makes a glad father, but a foolish man despises his mother. Folly is a joy to him who lacks sense, but a man of understanding walks straight ahead.

15:23   To make an apt answer is a joy to a man, and a word in season, how good it is!

15:30   The light of the eyes rejoices the heart, and good news refreshes the bones.

16:7   When a man's ways please the Lord, he makes even his enemies to be at peace with him.

16:24   Gracious words are like a honeycomb, sweetness to the soul and health to the body.

17:1   Better is a dry morsel with quiet than a house full of feasting with strife.

17:21–22   He who sires a fool gets himself sorrow, and the father of a fool has no joy. A joyful heart is good medicine, but a crushed spirit dries up the bones.

18:14   A man's spirit will endure sickness, but a crushed spirit who can bear?

21:15   When justice is done, it is a joy to the righteous but terror to evildoers.

23:15   My son, if your heart is wise, my heart too will be glad.

23:24–25   The father of the righteous will greatly rejoice; he who fathers a wise son will be glad in him. Let your father and mother be glad; let her who bore you rejoice.

24:17   Do not rejoice when your enemy falls, and let not your heart be glad when he stumbles,

25:20   Whoever sings songs to a heavy heart is like one who takes off a garment on a cold day, and like vinegar on soda.

25:25   Like cold water to a thirsty soul, so is good news from a far country.

27:7   One who is full loathes honey, but to one who is hungry everything bitter is sweet.

27:9   Oil and perfume make the heart glad, and the sweetness of a friend comes from his earnest counsel.

27:11   Be wise, my son, and make my heart glad, that I may answer him who reproaches me.

27:18   Whoever tends a fig tree will eat its fruit, and he who guards his master will be honored.

29:3   He who loves wisdom makes his father glad, but a companion of prostitutes squanders his wealth.

Heart/Mind

3:1   My son, do not forget my teaching, but let your heart keep my commandments.

3:3   Let not steadfast love and faithfulness forsake you; bind them around your neck; write them on the tablet of your heart.

3:5   Trust in the Lord with all your heart, and do not lean on your own understanding.

4:4   He taught me and said to me, "Let your heart hold fast my words; keep my commandments, and live."

4:21   Let them not escape from your sight; keep them within your heart.

4:23   Keep your heart with all vigilance, for from it flow the springs of life.

5:12   And you say, "How I hated discipline, and my heart despised reproof!"

6:14   With perverted heart devises evil, continually sowing discord.

6:18   A heart that devises wicked plans, feet that make haste to run to evil.

6:21   Bind them on your heart always; tie them around your neck.

6:25   Do not desire her beauty in your heart, and do not let her capture you with her eyelashes.

7:3   Bind them on your fingers; write them on the tablet of your heart.

7:10   And behold, the woman meets him, dressed as a prostitute, wily of heart.

7:25   Let not your heart turn aside to her ways; do not stray into her paths.

10:8   The wise of heart will receive commandments, but a babbling fool will come to ruin.

10:20   The tongue of the righteous is choice silver; the heart of the wicked is of little worth.

11:20   Those of crooked heart are an abomination to the Lord, but those of blameless ways are his delight.

12:8   A man is commended according to his good sense, but one of twisted mind is despised.

12:20   Deceit is in the heart of those who devise evil, but those who plan peace have joy.

12:23   A prudent man conceals knowledge, but the heart of fools proclaims folly.

12:25   Anxiety in a man's heart weighs him down, but a good word makes him glad.

13:12   Hope deferred makes the heart sick, but a desire fulfilled is a tree of life.

14:10   The heart knows its own bitterness, and no stranger shares its joy.

14:13   Even in laughter the heart may ache, and the end of joy may be grief.

14:14   The backslider in heart will be filled with the fruit of his ways, and a good man will be filled with the fruit of his ways.

14:30   A tranquil heart gives life to the flesh, but envy makes the bones rot.

14:33   Wisdom rests in the heart of a man of understanding, but it makes itself known even in the midst of fools.

15:11   Sheol and Abaddon lie open before the Lord; how much more the hearts of the children of man!

15:13–15   A glad heart makes a cheerful face, but by sorrow of heart the spirit is crushed. The heart of him who has understanding seeks knowledge, but the mouths of fools feed on folly. All the days of the afflicted are evil, but the cheerful of heart has a continual feast.

15:28   The heart of the righteous ponders how to answer, but the mouth of the wicked pours out evil things.

15:30   The light of the eyes rejoices the heart, and good news refreshes the bones.

16:1   The plans of the heart belong to man, but the answer of the tongue is from the Lord.

16:5   Everyone who is arrogant in heart is an abomination to the Lord; be assured, he will not go unpunished.

16:9   The heart of man plans his way, but the Lord establishes his steps.

16:21   The wise of heart is called discerning, and sweetness of speech increases persuasiveness.

16:23   The heart of the wise makes his speech judicious and adds persuasiveness to his lips.

17:3   The crucible is for silver, and the furnace is for gold, and the Lord tests hearts.

17:20   A man of crooked heart does not discover good, and one with a dishonest tongue falls into calamity.

17:22   A joyful heart is good medicine, but a crushed spirit dries up the bones.

18:2   A fool takes no pleasure in understanding, but only in expressing his opinion.

18:12   Before destruction a man's heart is haughty, but humility comes before honor.

18:15   An intelligent heart acquires knowledge, and the ear of the wise seeks knowledge.

19:3   When a man's folly brings his way to ruin, his heart rages against the Lord.

19:21   Many are the plans in the mind of a man, but it is the purpose of the Lord that will stand.

20:5   The purpose in a man's heart is like deep water, but a man of understanding will draw it out.

20:9   Who can say, "I have made my heart pure; I am clean from my sin"?

21:1   The king's heart is a stream of water in the hand of the Lord; he turns it wherever he will.

21:4   Haughty eyes and a proud heart, the lamp of the wicked, are sin.

22:11   He who loves purity of heart, and whose speech is gracious, will have the king as his friend.

22:15   Folly is bound up in the heart of a child, but the rod of discipline drives it far from him.

22:17   Incline your ear, and hear the words of the wise, and apply your heart to my knowledge.

23:7   For he is like one who is inwardly calculating. "Eat and drink!" he says to you, but his heart is not with you.

23:12   Apply your heart to instruction and your ear to words of knowledge.

23:15   My son, if your heart is wise, my heart too will be glad.

23:17–21   Let not your heart envy sinners, but continue in the fear of the Lord all the day. Surely there is a future, and your hope will not be cut off. Hear, my son, and be wise, and direct your heart in the way. Be not among drunkards or among gluttonous eaters of meat, for the drunkard and the glutton will come to poverty, and slumber will clothe them with rags.

23:26   My son, give me your heart, and let your eyes observe my ways.

23:33   Your eyes will see strange things, and your heart utter perverse things.

24:17   Do not rejoice when your enemy falls, and let not your heart be glad when he stumbles.

25:3   As the heavens for height, and the earth for depth, so the heart of kings is unsearchable.

25:20   Whoever sings songs to a heavy heart is like one who takes off a garment on a cold day, and like vinegar on soda.

26:23–25   Like the glaze covering an earthen vessel are fervent lips with an evil heart. Whoever hates disguises himself with his lips and harbors deceit in his heart; when he speaks graciously, believe him not, for there are seven abominations in his heart.

27:9   Oil and perfume make the heart glad, and the sweetness of a friend comes from his earnest counsel.

27:11   Be wise, my son, and make my heart glad, that I may answer him who reproaches me.

27:19   As in water face reflects face, so the heart of man reflects the man.

28:14   Blessed is the one who fears the Lord always, but whoever hardens his heart will fall into calamity.

28:26   Whoever trusts in his own mind is a fool, but he who walks in wisdom will be delivered.

31:11   The heart of her husband trusts in her, and he will have no lack of gain.

Honor

3:9   Honor the Lord with your wealth and with the firstfruits of all your produce.

3:16   Long life is in her right hand; in her left hand are riches and honor.

3:35   The wise will inherit honor, but fools get disgrace.

4:8–9   Prize her highly, and she will exalt you; she will honor you if you embrace her. She will place on your head a graceful garland; she will bestow on you a beautiful crown.

8:18   Riches and honor are with me, enduring wealth and righteousness.

11:16   A gracious woman gets honor, and violent men get riches.

12:9   Better to be lowly and have a servant than to play the great man and lack bread.

14:31   Whoever oppresses a poor man insults his Maker, but he who is generous to the needy honors him.

15:33   The fear of the Lord is instruction in wisdom, and humility comes before honor.

18:12   Before destruction a man's heart is haughty, but humility comes before honor.

20:3   It is an honor for a man to keep aloof from strife, but every fool will be quarreling.

20:29   The glory of young men is their strength, but the splendor of old men is their gray hair.

21:21   Whoever pursues righteousness and kindness will find life, righteousness, and honor.

22:4   The reward for humility and fear of the Lord is riches and honor and life.

25:6   Do not put yourself forward in the king's presence or stand in the place of the great.

26:1   Like snow in summer or rain in harvest, so honor is not fitting for a fool.

26:8   Like one who binds the stone in the sling is one who gives honor to a fool.

27:2   Let another praise you, and not your own mouth; a stranger, and not your own lips.

27:18   Whoever tends a fig tree will eat its fruit, and he who guards his master will be honored.

27:21   The crucible is for silver, and the furnace is for gold, and a man is tested by his praise.

29:23   One's pride will bring him low, but he who is lowly in spirit will obtain honor.

Humility

11:2   When pride comes, then comes disgrace, but with the humble is wisdom.

15:33   The fear of the Lord is instruction in wisdom, and humility comes before honor.

16:19   It is better to be of a lowly spirit with the poor than to divide the spoil with the proud.

18:12   Before destruction a man's heart is haughty, but humility comes before honor.

22:4   The reward for humility and fear of the Lord is riches and honor and life.

25:6–7   Do not put yourself forward in the king's presence or stand in the place of the great, for it is better to be told, "Come up here," than to be put lower in the presence of a noble.

25:27   It is not good to eat much honey, nor is it glorious to seek one's own glory.

27:1–2   Do not boast about tomorrow, for you do not know what a day may bring. Let another praise you, and not your own mouth; a stranger, and not your own lips.

29:23   One's pride will bring him low, but he who is lowly in spirit will obtain honor.

Love/Hate

1:22   How long, O simple ones, will you love being simple? How long will scoffers delight in their scoffing and fools hate knowledge?

1:29   Because they hated knowledge and did not choose the fear of the Lord.

3:12   For the Lord reproves him whom he loves, as a father the son in whom he delights.

4:6   Do not forsake her, and she will keep you; love her, and she will guard you.

5:12   And you say, "How I hated discipline, and my heart despised reproof!"

5:19   A lovely deer, a graceful doe. Let her breasts fill you at all times with delight; be intoxicated always in her love.

6:16   There are six things that the Lord hates, seven that are an abomination to him.

7:18   Come, let us take our fill of love till morning; let us delight ourselves with love.

8:13   The fear of the Lord is hatred of evil. Pride and arrogance and the way of evil and perverted speech I hate.

8:17   I love those who love me, and those who seek me diligently find me.

8:21   Granting an inheritance to those who love me, and filling their treasuries.

8:36   But he who fails to find me injures himself; all who hate me love death.

9:8   Do not reprove a scoffer, or he will hate you; reprove a wise man, and he will love you.

10:12   Hatred stirs up strife, but love covers all offenses.

11:15   Whoever puts up security for a stranger will surely suffer harm, but he who hates striking hands in pledge is secure.

12:1   Whoever loves discipline loves knowledge, but he who hates reproof is stupid.

13:5   The righteous hates falsehood, but the wicked brings shame and disgrace.

13:24   Whoever spares the rod hates his son, but he who loves him is diligent to discipline him.

14:17   A man of quick temper acts foolishly, and a man of evil devices is hated.

14:20   The poor is disliked even by his neighbor, but the rich has many friends.

15:9   The way of the wicked is an abomination to the Lord, but he loves him who pursues righteousness.

15:10   There is severe discipline for him who forsakes the way; whoever hates reproof will die.

15:12   A scoffer does not like to be reproved; he will not go to the wise.

15:17   Better is a dinner of herbs where love is than a fattened ox and hatred with it.

15:27   Whoever is greedy for unjust gain troubles his own household, but he who hates bribes will live.

16:13   Righteous lips are the delight of a king, and he loves him who speaks what is right.

17:9   Whoever covers an offense seeks love, but he who repeats a matter separates close friends.

17:17   A friend loves at all times, and a brother is born for adversity.

17:19   Whoever loves transgression loves strife; he who makes his door high seeks destruction.

18:21   Death and life are in the power of the tongue, and those who love it will eat its fruits.

19:7   All a poor man's brothers hate him; how much more do his friends go far from him! He pursues them with words, but does not have them.

19:8   Whoever gets sense loves his own soul; he who keeps understanding will discover good.

20:13   Love not sleep, lest you come to poverty; open your eyes, and you will have plenty of bread.

21:17   Whoever loves pleasure will be a poor man; he who loves wine and oil will not be rich.

22:11   He who loves purity of heart, and whose speech is gracious, will have the king as his friend.

25:17   Let your foot be seldom in your neighbor's house, lest he have his fill of you and hate you.

26:24   Whoever hates disguises himself with his lips and harbors deceit in his heart.

26:28   A lying tongue hates its victims, and a flattering mouth works ruin.

27:5   Better is open rebuke than hidden love.

28:16   A ruler who lacks understanding is a cruel oppressor, but he who hates unjust gain will prolong his days.

29:3   He who loves wisdom makes his father glad, but a companion of prostitutes squanders his wealth.

29:10   Bloodthirsty men hate one who is blameless and seek the life of the upright.

29:24   The partner of a thief hates his own life; he hears the curse, but discloses nothing.

Lying/Deceiving

4:24   Put away from you crooked speech, and put devious talk far from you.

6:12   A worthless person, a wicked man, goes about with crooked speech.

6:17   Haughty eyes, a lying tongue, and hands that shed innocent blood.

6:19   A false witness who breathes out lies, and one who sows discord among brothers.

10:18   The one who conceals hatred has lying lips, and whoever utters slander is a fool.

11:1   A false balance is an abomination to the Lord, but a just weight is his delight.

11:3   The integrity of the upright guides them, but the crookedness of the treacherous destroys them.

11:18   The wicked earns deceptive wages, but one who sows righteousness gets a sure reward.

12:5   The thoughts of the righteous are just; the counsels of the wicked are deceitful.

12:17   Whoever speaks the truth gives honest evidence, but a false witness utters deceit.

12:19–20   Truthful lips endure forever, but a lying tongue is but for a moment. Deceit is in the heart of those who devise evil, but those who plan peace have joy.

12:22   Lying lips are an abomination to the Lord, but those who act faithfully are his delight.

13:5   The righteous hates falsehood, but the wicked brings shame and disgrace.

14:5   A faithful witness does not lie, but a false witness breathes out lies.

14:8   The wisdom of the prudent is to discern his way, but the folly of fools is deceiving.

14:25   A truthful witness saves lives, but one who breathes out lies is deceitful.

17:4   An evildoer listens to wicked lips, and a liar gives ear to a mischievous tongue.

17:7   Fine speech is not becoming to a fool; still less is false speech to a prince.

19:5   A false witness will not go unpunished, and he who breathes out lies will not escape.

19:9   A false witness will not go unpunished, and he who breathes out lies will perish.

19:22   What is desired in a man is steadfast love, and a poor man is better than a liar.

19:28   A worthless witness mocks at justice, and the mouth of the wicked devours iniquity.

20:17   Bread gained by deceit is sweet to a man, but afterward his mouth will be full of gravel.

20:23   Unequal weights are an abomination to the Lord, and false scales are not good.

21:6   The getting of treasures by a lying tongue is a fleeting vapor and a snare of death.

21:28   A false witness will perish, but the word of a man who hears will endure.

23:3   Do not desire his delicacies, for they are deceptive food.

24:28   Be not a witness against your neighbor without cause, and do not deceive with your lips.

25:14   Like clouds and wind without rain is a man who boasts of a gift he does not give.

25:18   A man who bears false witness against his neighbor is like a war club, or a sword, or a sharp arrow.

26:18–19   Like a madman who throws firebrands, arrows, and death is the man who deceives his neighbor and says, "I am only joking!"

26:24   Whoever hates disguises himself with his lips and harbors deceit in his heart.

27:6   Faithful are the wounds of a friend; profuse are the kisses of an enemy.

29:12   If a ruler listens to falsehood, all his officials will be wicked.

29:24   The partner of a thief hates his own life; he hears the curse, but discloses nothing.

30:6   Do not add to his words, lest he rebuke you and you be found a liar.

30:8   Remove far from me falsehood and lying; give me neither poverty nor riches; feed me with the food that is needful for me.

31:30   Charm is deceitful, and beauty is vain, but a woman who fears the Lord is to be praised.

Morality/Immorality

Morality

5:15–20   Drink water from your own cistern, flowing water from your own well. Should your springs be scattered abroad, streams of water in the streets? Let them be for yourself alone, and not for strangers with you. Let your fountain be blessed, and rejoice in the wife of your youth, a lovely deer, a graceful doe. Let her breasts fill you at all times with delight; be intoxicated always in her love. Why should you be intoxicated, my son, with a forbidden woman and embrace the bosom of an adulteress?

Immorality

2:16–19   So you will be delivered from the forbidden woman, from the adulteress with her smooth words, who forsakes the companion of her youth and forgets the covenant of her God; for her house sinks down to death, and her paths to the departed; none who go to her come back, nor do they regain the paths of life.

5:3–14   For the lips of a forbidden woman drip honey, and her speech is smoother than oil, but in the end she is bitter as wormwood, sharp as a two–edged sword. Her feet go down to death; her steps follow the path to Sheol; she does not ponder the path of life; her ways wander, and she does not know it. And now, O sons, listen to me, and do not depart from the words of my mouth. Keep your way far from her, and do not go near the door of her house, lest you give your honor to others and your years to the merciless, lest strangers take their fill of your strength, and your labors go to the house of a foreigner, and at the end of your life you groan, when your flesh and body are consumed, and you say, "How I hated discipline, and my heart despised reproof! I did not listen to the voice of my teachers or incline my ear to my instructors. I am at the brink of utter ruin in the assembled congregation."

5:20   Why should you be intoxicated, my son, with a forbidden woman and embrace the bosom of an adulteress?

6:24–35   To preserve you from the evil woman, from the smooth tongue of the adulteress. Do not desire her beauty in your heart, and do not let her capture you with her eyelashes; for the price of a prostitute is only a loaf of bread, but a married woman hunts down a precious life. Can a man carry fire next to his chest and his clothes not be burned? Or can one walk on hot coals and his feet not be scorched? So is he who goes in to his neighbor's wife; none who touches her will go unpunished. People do not despise a thief if he steals to satisfy his appetite when he is hungry, but if he is caught, he will pay sevenfold; he will give all the goods of his house. He who commits adultery lacks sense; he who does it destroys himself. Wounds and dishonor will he get, and his disgrace will not be wiped away. For jealousy makes a man furious, and he will not spare when he takes revenge. He will accept no compensation; he will refuse though you multiply gifts.

7:5–27 To keep you from the forbidden woman, from the adulteress with her smooth words. For at the window of my house I have looked out through my lattice, and I have seen among the simple, I have perceived among the youths, a young man lacking sense, passing along the street near her corner, taking the road to her house in the twilight, in the evening, at the time of night and darkness. And behold, the woman meets him, dressed as a prostitute, wily of heart. She is loud and wayward; her feet do not stay at home; now in the street, now in the market, and at every corner she lies in wait. She seizes him and kisses him, and with bold face she says to him, "I had to offer sacrifices, and today I have paid my vows; so now I have come out to meet you, to seek you eagerly, and I have found you. I have spread my couch with coverings, colored linens from Egyptian linen; I have perfumed my bed with myrrh, aloes, and cinnamon. Come, let us take our fill of love till morning; let us delight ourselves with love. For my husband is not at home; he has gone on a long journey; he took a bag of money with him; at full moon he will come home." With much seductive speech she persuades him; with her smooth talk she compels him. All at once he follows her, as an ox goes to the slaughter, or as a stag is caught fast till an arrow pierces its liver; as a bird rushes into a snare; he does not know that it will cost him his life. And now, O sons, listen to me, and be attentive to the words of my mouth. Let not your heart turn aside to her ways; do not stray into her paths, for many a victim has she laid low, and all her slain are a mighty throng. Her house is the way to Sheol, going down to the chambers of death.

9:13–18 The woman Folly is loud; she is seductive and knows nothing. She sits at the door of her house; she takes a seat on the highest places of the town, calling to those who pass by, who are going straight on their way, "Whoever is simple, let him turn in here!" And to him who lacks sense she says, "Stolen water is sweet, and bread eaten in secret is pleasant." But he does not know that the dead are there, that her guests are in the depths of Sheol.

11:22   Like a gold ring in a pig's snout is a beautiful woman without discretion.

22:14   The mouth of forbidden women is a deep pit; he with whom the Lord is angry will fall into it.

23:26–28   My son, give me your heart, and let your eyes observe my ways. For a prostitute is a deep pit; an adulteress is a narrow well. She lies in wait like a robber and increases the traitors among mankind.

27:13   Take a man's garment when he has put up security for a stranger, and hold it in pledge when he puts up security for an adulteress.

29:3   He who loves wisdom makes his father glad, but a companion of prostitutes squanders his wealth.

30:18–20   Three things are too wonderful for me; four I do not understand: the way of an eagle in the sky, the way of a serpent on a rock, the way of a ship on the high seas, and the way of a man with a virgin. This is the way of an adulteress: she eats and wipes her mouth and says, "I have done no wrong."

31:2–3   What are you doing, my son? What are you doing, son of my womb? What are you doing, son of my vows? Do not give your strength to women, your ways to those who destroy kings.

Plans/Desires/Ways

1:19   Such are the ways of everyone who is greedy for unjust gain; it takes away the life of its possessors.

1:31   Therefore they shall eat the fruit of their way, and have their fill of their own devices.

2:8   Guarding the paths of justice and watching over the way of his saints.

2:12–13   Delivering you from the way of evil, from men of perverted speech, who forsake the paths of uprightness to walk in the ways of darkness.

2:15   Men whose paths are crooked, and who are devious in their ways.

2:20   So you will walk in the way of the good and keep to the paths of the righteous.

3:5–6   Trust in the Lord with all your heart, and do not lean on your own understanding. In all your ways acknowledge him, and he will make straight your paths.

3:17   Her ways are ways of pleasantness, and all her paths are peace.

3:23   Then you will walk on your way securely, and your foot will not stumble.

3:31   Do not envy a man of violence and do not choose any of his ways.

4:11–12   I have taught you the way of wisdom; I have led you in the paths of uprightness. When you walk, your step will not be hampered, and if you run, you will not stumble.

4:14   Do not enter the path of the wicked, and do not walk in the way of the evil.

4:19   The way of the wicked is like deep darkness; they do not know over what they stumble.

4:26   Ponder the path of your feet; then all your ways will be sure.

5:5   Her feet go down to death; her steps follow the path to Sheol.

5:6   She does not ponder the path of life; her ways wander, and she does not know it.

5:8   Keep your way far from her, and do not go near the door of her house.

5:21   For a man's ways are before the eyes of the Lord, and he ponders all his paths.

6:6   Go to the ant, O sluggard; consider her ways, and be wise.

6:18   A heart that devises wicked plans, feet that make haste to run to evil.

6:23   For the commandment is a lamp and the teaching a light, and the reproofs of discipline are the way of life.

7:25   Let not your heart turn aside to her ways; do not stray into her paths.

8:13   The fear of the Lord is hatred of evil. Pride and arrogance and the way of evil and perverted speech I hate.

8:20   I walk in the way of righteousness, in the paths of justice.

8:32   And now, O sons, listen to me: blessed are those who keep my ways.

9:6   Leave your simple ways, and live, and walk in the way of insight.

10:9   Whoever walks in integrity walks securely, but he who makes his ways crooked will be found out.

10:29   The way of the Lord is a stronghold to the blameless, but destruction to evildoers.

11:5   The righteousness of the blameless keeps his way straight, but the wicked falls by his own wickedness.

11:14   Where there is no guidance, a people falls, but in an abundance of counselors there is safety.

11:20   Those of crooked heart are an abomination to the Lord, but those of blameless ways are his delight.

12:15   The way of a fool is right in his own eyes, but a wise man listens to advice.

12:26   One who is righteous is a guide to his neighbor, but the way of the wicked leads them astray.

12:28   In the path of righteousness is life, and in its pathway there is no death.

13:6   Righteousness guards him whose way is blameless, but sin overthrows the wicked.

13:15   Good sense wins favor, but the way of the treacherous is their ruin.

14:2   Whoever walks in uprightness fears the Lord, but he who is devious in his ways despises him.

14:8   The wisdom of the prudent is to discern his way, but the folly of fools is deceiving.

14:12   There is a way that seems right to a man, but its end is the way to death.

14:14   The backslider in heart will be filled with the fruit of his ways, and a good man will be filled with the fruit of his ways.

14:15   The simple believes everything, but the prudent gives thought to his steps.

15:9–10   The way of the wicked is an abomination to the Lord, but he loves him who pursues righteousness. There is severe discipline for him who forsakes the way; whoever hates reproof will die.

15:19   The way of a sluggard is like a hedge of thorns, but the path of the upright is a level highway.

15:22   Without counsel plans fail, but with many advisers they succeed.

16:1–3   The plans of the heart belong to man, but the answer of the tongue is from the Lord. All the ways of a man are pure in his own eyes, but the Lord weighs the spirit. Commit your work to the Lord, and your plans will be established.

16:7   When a man's ways please the Lord, he makes even his enemies to be at peace with him.

16:9   The heart of man plans his way, but the Lord establishes his steps.

16:17   The highway of the upright turns aside from evil; whoever guards his way preserves his life.

16:25   There is a way that seems right to a man, but its end is the way to death.

16:29   A man of violence entices his neighbor and leads him in a way that is not good.

16:33   The lot is cast into the lap, but its every decision is from the Lord.

17:23   The wicked accepts a bribe in secret to pervert the ways of justice.

19:2–3   Desire without knowledge is not good, and whoever makes haste with his feet misses his way. When a man's folly brings his way to ruin, his heart rages against the Lord.

19:16   Whoever keeps the commandment keeps his life; he who despises his ways will die.

19:21   Many are the plans in the mind of a man, but it is the purpose of the Lord that will stand.

20:5   The purpose in a man's heart is like deep water, but a man of understanding will draw it out.

20:14   "Bad, Bad," says the buyer, but when he goes away, then he boasts.

20:18   Plans are established by counsel; by wise guidance wage war.

20:24   A man's steps are from the Lord; how then can man understand his way?

21:2   Every way of a man is right in his own eyes, but the Lord weighs the heart.

21:5   The plans of the diligent lead surely to abundance, but everyone who is hasty comes only to poverty.

21:8   The way of the guilty is crooked, but the conduct of the pure is upright.

21:16   One who wanders from the way of good sense will rest in the assembly of the dead.

21:29   A wicked man puts on a bold face, but the upright gives thought to his ways.

22:5   Thorns and snares are in the way of the crooked; whoever guards his soul will keep far from them.

22:6   Train up a child in the way he should go; even when he is old he will not depart from it.

22:25   Lest you learn his ways and entangle yourself in a snare.

23:19   Hear, my son, and be wise, and direct your heart in the way.

23:26   My son, give me your heart, and let your eyes observe my ways.

24:6   For by wise guidance you can wage your war, and in abundance of counselors there is victory.

24:8   Whoever plans to do evil will be called a schemer.

28:10   Whoever misleads the upright into an evil way will fall into his own pit, but the blameless will have a goodly inheritance.

29:27   An unjust man is an abomination to the righteous, but one whose way is straight is an abomination to the wicked.

30:19–20   The way of an eagle in the sky, the way of a serpent on a rock, the way of a ship on the high seas, and the way of a man with a virgin. This is the way of an adulteress: she eats and wipes her mouth and says, "I have done no wrong."

31:3   Do not give your strength to women, your ways to those who destroy kings.

Pride

1:22   How long, O simple ones, will you love being simple? How long will scoffers delight in their scoffing and fools hate knowledge?

3:34   Toward the scorners he is scornful, but to the humble he gives favor.

6:16–17   There are six things that the Lord hates, seven that are an abomination to him: haughty eyes, a lying tongue, and hands that shed innocent blood.

8:13   The fear of the Lord is hatred of evil. Pride and arrogance and the way of evil and perverted speech I hate.

9:7–8   Whoever corrects a scoffer gets himself abuse, and he who reproves a wicked man incurs injury. Do not reprove a scoffer, or he will hate you; reprove a wise man, and he will love you.

11:2   When pride comes, then comes disgrace, but with the humble is wisdom.

12:9   Better to be lowly and have a servant than to play the great man and lack bread.

13:1   A wise son hears his father's instruction, but a scoffer does not listen to rebuke.

13:10   By insolence comes nothing but strife, but with those who take advice is wisdom.

14:6   A scoffer seeks wisdom in vain, but knowledge is easy for a man of understanding.

14:16   One who is wise is cautious and turns away from evil, but a fool is reckless and careless.

15:12   A scoffer does not like to be reproved; he will not go to the wise.

15:25 The Lord tears down the house of the proud but maintains the widow's boundaries.

16:5 Everyone who is arrogant in heart is an abomination to the Lord; be assured, he will not go unpunished.

16:18–19 Pride goes before destruction, and a haughty spirit before a fall. It is better to be of a lowly spirit with the poor than to divide the spoil with the proud.

18:12 Before destruction a man's heart is haughty, but humility comes before honor.

19:25 Strike a scoffer, and the simple will learn prudence; reprove a man of understanding, and he will gain knowledge.

19:29 Condemnation is ready for scoffers, and beating for the backs of fools.

21:4 Haughty eyes and a proud heart, the lamp of the wicked, are sin.

21:11 When a scoffer is punished, the simple becomes wise; when a wise man is instructed, he gains knowledge.

21:24 "Scoffer" is the name of the arrogant, haughty man who acts with arrogant pride.

22:10 Drive out a scoffer, and strife will go out, and quarreling and abuse will cease.

24:9 The devising of folly is sin, and the scoffer is an abomination to mankind.

25:6–7 Do not put yourself forward in the king's presence or stand in the place of the great, for it is better to be told, "Come up here," than to be put lower in the presence of a noble.

25:14 Like clouds and wind without rain is a man who boasts of a gift he does not give.

25:27 It is not good to eat much honey, nor is it glorious to seek one's own glory.

27:1–2 Do not boast about tomorrow, for you do not know what a day may bring. Let another praise you, and not your own mouth; a stranger, and not your own lips.

28:25 A greedy man stirs up strife, but the one who trusts in the Lord will be enriched.

29:23   One's pride will bring him low, but he who is lowly in spirit will obtain honor.

Priorities

3:13–14   Blessed is the one who finds wisdom, and the one who gets understanding, for the gain from her is better than gain from silver and her profit better than gold.

8:11   For wisdom is better than jewels, and all that you may desire cannot compare with her.

8:19   My fruit is better than gold, even fine gold, and my yield than choice silver.

12:9   Better to be lowly and have a servant than to play the great man and lack bread.

15:16   Better is a little with the fear of the Lord than great treasure and trouble with it.

15:17   Better is a dinner of herbs where love is than a fattened ox and hatred with it.

16:8   Better is a little with righteousness than great revenues with injustice.

16:16   How much better to get wisdom than gold! To get understanding is to be chosen rather than silver.

16:19   It is better to be of a lowly spirit with the poor than to divide the spoil with the proud.

16:32   Whoever is slow to anger is better than the mighty, and he who rules his spirit than he who takes a city.

17:1   Better is a dry morsel with quiet than a house full of feasting with strife.

19:1   Better is a poor person who walks in his integrity than one who is crooked in speech and is a fool.

19:22   What is desired in a man is steadfast love, and a poor man is better than a liar.

21:9   It is better to live in a corner of the housetop than in a house shared with a quarrelsome wife.

21:19   It is better to live in a desert land than with a quarrelsome and fretful woman.

22:1   A good name is to be chosen rather than great riches, and favor is better than silver or gold.

23:4–5   Do not toil to acquire wealth; be discerning enough to desist. When your eyes light on it, it is gone, for suddenly it sprouts wings, flying like an eagle toward heaven.

25:7   For it is better to be told, "Come up here," than to be put lower in the presence of a noble.

25:24   It is better to live in a corner of the housetop than in a house shared with a quarrelsome wife.

27:5   Better is open rebuke than hidden love.

27:10   Do not forsake your friend and your father's friend, and do not go to your brother's house in the day of your calamity. Better is a neighbor who is near than a brother who is far away.

28:6   Better is a poor man who walks in his integrity than a rich man who is crooked in his ways.

Serving

11:29   Whoever troubles his own household will inherit the wind, and the fool will be servant to the wise of heart.

12:9   Better to be lowly and have a servant than to play the great man and lack bread.

14:35   A servant who deals wisely has the king's favor, but his wrath falls on one who acts shamefully.

17:2   A servant who deals wisely will rule over a son who acts shamefully and will share the inheritance as one of the brothers.

19:10   It is not fitting for a fool to live in luxury, much less for a slave to rule over princes.

22:7   The rich rules over the poor, and the borrower is the slave of the lender.

25:13   Like the cold of snow in the time of harvest is a faithful messenger to those who send him; he refreshes the soul of his masters.

27:18   Whoever tends a fig tree will eat its fruit, and he who guards his master will be honored.

29:19   By mere words a servant is not disciplined, for though he understands, he will not respond.

29:21   Whoever pampers his servant from childhood will in the end find him his heir.

30:10   Do not slander a servant to his master, lest he curse you and you be held guilty.

30:22   A slave when he becomes king, and a fool when he is filled with food.

Testing

16:2   All the ways of a man are pure in his own eyes, but the Lord weighs the spirit.

17:3   The crucible is for silver, and the furnace is for gold, and the Lord tests hearts.

18:17   The one who states his case first seems right, until the other comes and examines him.

21:2   Every way of a man is right in his own eyes, but the Lord weighs the heart.

24:12   If you say, "Behold, we did not know this," does not he who weighs the heart perceive it? Does not he who keeps watch over your soul know it, and will he not repay man according to his work?

25:4   Take away the dross from the silver, and the smith has material for a vessel.

27:17   Iron sharpens iron, and one man sharpens another.

27:21   The crucible is for silver, and the furnace is for gold, and a man is tested by his praise.

28:23   Whoever rebukes a man will afterward find more favor than he who flatters with his tongue.

30:5   Every word of God proves true; he is a shield to those who take refuge in him.

Tongue/Words/Listening

1:5   Let the wise hear and increase in learning, and the one who understands obtain guidance.

1:6   To understand a proverb and a saying, the words of the wise and their riddles.

1:8   Hear, my son, your father's instruction, and forsake not your mother's teaching.

1:23   If you turn at my reproof, behold, I will pour out my spirit to you; I will make my words known to you.

2:2   Making your ear attentive to wisdom and inclining your heart to understanding.

2:6   For the Lord gives wisdom; from his mouth come knowledge and understanding.

2:12   Delivering you from the way of evil, from men of perverted speech.

2:16   So you will be delivered from the forbidden woman, from the adulteress with her smooth words.

4:1   Hear, O sons, a father's instruction, and be attentive, that you may gain insight.

4:4–5   He taught me and said to me, "Let your heart hold fast my words; keep my commandments, and live. Get wisdom; get insight; do not forget, and do not turn away from the words of my mouth."

4:10   Hear, my son, and accept my words, that the years of your life may be many.

4:20   My son, be attentive to my words; incline your ear to my sayings.

4:24   Put away from you crooked speech, and put devious talk far from you.

5:1–2   My son, be attentive to my wisdom; incline your ear to my understanding, that you may keep discretion, and your lips may guard knowledge.

5:3   For the lips of a forbidden woman drip honey, and her speech is smoother than oil.

5:7   And now, O sons, listen to me, and do not depart from the words of my mouth.

5:13–14   "I did not listen to the voice of my teachers or incline my ear to my instructors. I am at the brink of utter ruin in the assembled congregation."

6:2   If you are snared in the words of your mouth, caught in the words of your mouth.

6:12   A worthless person, a wicked man, goes about with crooked speech.

6:17   Haughty eyes, a lying tongue, and hands that shed innocent blood.

6:19   A false witness who breathes out lies, and one who sows discord among brothers.

6:22   When you walk, they will lead you; when you lie down, they will watch over you; and when you awake, they will talk with you.

6:24   To preserve you from the evil woman, from the smooth tongue of the adulteress.

7:1   My son, keep my words and treasure up my commandments within you.

7:5   To keep you from the forbidden woman, from the adulteress with her smooth words.

7:21   With much seductive speech she persuades him; with her smooth talk she compels him.

7:24   And now, O sons, listen to me, and be attentive to the words of my mouth.

8:6–8   Hear, for I will speak noble things, and from my lips will come what is right, for my mouth will utter truth; wickedness is an abomination to my lips. All the words of my mouth are righteous; there is nothing twisted or crooked in them.

8:13   The fear of the Lord is hatred of evil. Pride and arrogance and the way of evil and perverted speech I hate.

8:32   And now, O sons, listen to me: blessed are those who keep my ways.

10:6   Blessings are on the head of the righteous, but the mouth of the wicked conceals violence.

10:8   The wise of heart will receive commandments, but a babbling fool will come to ruin.

10:10   Whoever winks the eye causes trouble, but a babbling fool will come to ruin.

10:11   The mouth of the righteous is a fountain of life, but the mouth of the wicked conceals violence.

10:13   On the lips of him who has understanding, wisdom is found, but a rod is for the back of him who lacks sense.

10:14   The wise lay up knowledge, but the mouth of a fool brings ruin near.

10:18–21   The one who conceals hatred has lying lips, and whoever utters slander is a fool. When words are many, transgression is not lacking, but whoever restrains his lips is prudent. The tongue of the righteous is choice silver; the heart of the wicked is of little worth. The lips of the righteous feed many, but fools die for lack of sense.

10:31–32   The mouth of the righteous brings forth wisdom, but the perverse tongue will be cut off. The lips of the righteous know what is acceptable, but the mouth of the wicked, what is perverse.

11:9   With his mouth the godless man would destroy his neighbor, but by knowledge the righteous are delivered.

11:11–13   By the blessing of the upright a city is exalted, but by the mouth of the wicked it is overthrown. Whoever belittles his neighbor lacks sense, but a man of understanding remains silent. Whoever goes about slandering reveals secrets, but he who is trustworthy in spirit keeps a thing covered.

12:6   The words of the wicked lie in wait for blood, but the mouth of the upright delivers them.

12:13   An evil man is ensnared by the transgression of his lips, but the righteous escapes from trouble.

12:14   From the fruit of his mouth a man is satisfied with good, and the work of a man's hand comes back to him.

12:17–19   Whoever speaks the truth gives honest evidence, but a false witness utters deceit. There is one whose rash words are like sword thrusts, but the tongue of the wise brings healing. Truthful lips endure forever, but a lying tongue is but for a moment.

12:22 Lying lips are an abomination to the Lord, but those who act faithfully are his delight.

12:25 Anxiety in a man's heart weighs him down, but a good word makes him glad.

13:1 A wise son hears his father's instruction, but a scoffer does not listen to rebuke.

13:2–3 From the fruit of his mouth a man eats what is good, but the desire of the treacherous is for violence. Whoever guards his mouth preserves his life; he who opens wide his lips comes to ruin.

14:3 By the mouth of a fool comes a rod for his back, but the lips of the wise will preserve them.

14:5 A faithful witness does not lie, but a false witness breathes out lies.

14:7 Leave the presence of a fool, for there you do not meet words of knowledge.

14:23 In all toil there is profit, but mere talk tends only to poverty.

14:25 A truthful witness saves lives, but one who breathes out lies is deceitful.

15:1–2 A soft answer turns away wrath, but a harsh word stirs up anger. The tongue of the wise commends knowledge, but the mouths of fools pour out folly.

15:4 A gentle tongue is a tree of life, but perverseness in it breaks the spirit.

15:7 The lips of the wise spread knowledge; not so the hearts of fools.

15:14 The heart of him who has understanding seeks knowledge, but the mouths of fools feed on folly.

15:23 To make an apt answer is a joy to a man, and a word in season, how good it is!

15:26 The thoughts of the wicked are an abomination to the Lord, but gracious words are pure.

15:28   The heart of the righteous ponders how to answer, but the mouth of the wicked pours out evil things.

15:31   The ear that listens to life–giving reproof will dwell among the wise.

16:1   The plans of the heart belong to man, but the answer of the tongue is from the Lord.

16:10   An oracle is on the lips of a king; his mouth does not sin in judgment.

16:13   Righteous lips are the delight of a king, and he loves him who speaks what is right.

16:21   The wise of heart is called discerning, and sweetness of speech increases persuasiveness.

16:23–24   The heart of the wise makes his speech judicious and adds persuasiveness to his lips. Gracious words are like a honeycomb, sweetness to the soul and health to the body.

16:27–28   A worthless man plots evil, and his speech is like a scorching fire. A dishonest man spreads strife, and a whisperer separates close friends.

16:30   Whoever winks his eyes plans dishonest things; he who purses his lips brings evil to pass.

17:4   An evildoer listens to wicked lips, and a liar gives ear to a mischievous tongue.

17:7   Fine speech is not becoming to a fool; still less is false speech to a prince.

17:9   Whoever covers an offense seeks love, but he who repeats a matter separates close friends.

17:10   A rebuke goes deeper into a man of understanding than a hundred blows into a fool.

17:20   A man of crooked heart does not discover good, and one with a dishonest tongue falls into calamity.

17:27–28   Whoever restrains his words has knowledge, and he who has a cool spirit is a man of understanding. Even a fool who keeps silent is considered wise; when he closes his lips, he is deemed intelligent.

18:4   The words of a man's mouth are deep waters; the fountain of wisdom is a bubbling brook.

18:6–8   A fool's lips walk into a fight, and his mouth invites a beating. A fool's mouth is his ruin, and his lips are a snare to his soul. The words of a whisperer are like delicious morsels; they go down into the inner parts of the body.

18:13   If one gives an answer before he hears, it is his folly and shame.

18:15   An intelligent heart acquires knowledge, and the ear of the wise seeks knowledge.

18:20–21   From the fruit of a man's mouth his stomach is satisfied; he is satisfied by the yield of his lips. Death and life are in the power of the tongue, and those who love it will eat its fruits.

18:23   The poor use entreaties, but the rich answer roughly.

19:1   Better is a poor person who walks in his integrity than one who is crooked in speech and is a fool.

19:5   A false witness will not go unpunished, and he who breathes out lies will not escape.

19:7   All a poor man's brothers hate him; how much more do his friends go far from him! He pursues them with words, but does not have them.

19:9   A false witness will not go unpunished, and he who breathes out lies will perish.

19:20   Listen to advice and accept instruction, that you may gain wisdom in the future.

19:22   What is desired in a man is steadfast love, and a poor man is better than a liar.

19:27   Cease to hear instruction, my son, and you will stray from the words of knowledge.

19:28   A worthless witness mocks at justice, and the mouth of the wicked devours iniquity.

20:12   The hearing ear and the seeing eye, the Lord has made them both.

20:15   There is gold and abundance of costly stones, but the lips of knowledge are a precious jewel.

20:17   Bread gained by deceit is sweet to a man, but afterward his mouth will be full of gravel.

20:19   Whoever goes about slandering reveals secrets; therefore do not associate with a simple babbler.

20:25   It is a snare to say rashly, "It is holy," and to reflect only after making vows.

21:6   The getting of treasures by a lying tongue is a fleeting vapor and a snare of death.

21:13   Whoever closes his ear to the cry of the poor will himself call out and not be answered.

21:23   Whoever keeps his mouth and his tongue keeps himself out of trouble.

21:28   A false witness will perish, but the word of a man who hears will endure.

22:11–12   He who loves purity of heart, and whose speech is gracious, will have the king as his friend. The eyes of the Lord keep watch over knowledge, but he overthrows the words of the traitor.

22:14   The mouth of forbidden women is a deep pit; he with whom the Lord is angry will fall into it.

22:17–18   Incline your ear, and hear the words of the wise, and apply your heart to my knowledge, for it will be pleasant if you keep them within you, if all of them are ready on your lips.

22:20–21   Have I not written for you thirty sayings of counsel and knowledge, to make you know what is right and true, that you may give a true answer to those who sent you?

23:9   Do not speak in the hearing of a fool, for he will despise the good sense of your words.

23:12   Apply your heart to instruction and your ear to words of knowledge.

23:15–16   My son, if your heart is wise, my heart too will be glad. My inmost being will exult when your lips speak what is right.

23:19   Hear, my son, and be wise, and direct your heart in the way.

23:22   Listen to your father who gave you life, and do not despise your mother when she is old.

24:2   For their hearts devise violence, and their lips talk of trouble.

24:7   Wisdom is too high for a fool; in the gate he does not open his mouth.

24:25–26   But those who rebuke the wicked will have delight, and a good blessing will come upon them. Whoever gives an honest answer kisses the lips.

24:28–29   Be not a witness against your neighbor without cause, and do not deceive with your lips. Do not say, "I will do to him as he has done to me; I will pay the man back for what he has done."

25:8–11   Do not hastily bring into court, for what will you do in the end, when your neighbor puts you to shame? Argue your case with your neighbor himself, and do not reveal another's secret, lest he who hears you bring shame upon you, and your ill repute have no end. A word fitly spoken is like apples of gold in a setting of silver.

25:12   Like a gold ring or an ornament of gold is a wise reprover to a listening ear.

25:15   With patience a ruler may be persuaded, and a soft tongue will break a bone.

25:18   A man who bears false witness against his neighbor is like a war club, or a sword, or a sharp arrow.

25:23   The north wind brings forth rain, and a backbiting tongue, angry looks.

25:28   A man without self-control is like a city broken into and left without walls.

26:4–5   Answer not a fool according to his folly, lest you be like him yourself. Answer a fool according to his folly, lest he be wise in his own eyes.

26:7   Like a lame man's legs, which hang useless, is a proverb in the mouth of fools.

26:9   Like a thorn that goes up into the hand of a drunkard is a proverb in the mouth of fools.

26:15–16   The sluggard buries his hand in the dish; it wears him out to bring it back to his mouth. The sluggard is wiser in his own eyes than seven men who can answer sensibly.

26:20–28   For lack of wood the fire goes out, and where there is no whisperer, quarreling ceases. As charcoal to hot embers and wood to fire, so is a quarrelsome man for kindling strife. The words of a whisperer are like delicious morsels; they go down into the inner parts of the body. Like the glaze covering an earthen vessel are fervent lips with an evil heart. Whoever hates disguises himself with his lips and harbors deceit in his heart; when he speaks graciously, believe him not, for there are seven abominations in his heart; though his hatred be covered with deception, his wickedness will be exposed in the assembly. Whoever digs a pit will fall into it, and a stone will come back on him who starts it rolling. A lying tongue hates its victims, and a flattering mouth works ruin.

27:2   Let another praise you, and not your own mouth; a stranger, and not your own lips.

27:5   Better is open rebuke than hidden love.

28:9   If one turns away his ear from hearing the law, even his prayer is an abomination.

28:23   Whoever rebukes a man will afterward find more favor than he who flatters with his tongue.

29:5   A man who flatters his neighbor spreads a net for his feet.

29:19   By mere words a servant is not disciplined, for though he understands, he will not respond.

29:20   Do you see a man who is hasty in his words? There is more hope for a fool than for him.

30:6   Do not add to his words, lest he rebuke you and you be found a liar.

30:8   Remove far from me falsehood and lying; give me neither poverty nor riches; feed me with the food that is needful for me.

30:10   Do not slander a servant to his master, lest he curse you and you be held guilty.

30:32   If you have been foolish, exalting yourself, or if you have been devising evil, put your hand on your mouth.

31:8–9   Open your mouth for the mute, for the rights of all who are destitute. Open your mouth, judge righteously, defend the rights of the poor and needy.

31:26   She opens her mouth with wisdom, and the teaching of kindness is on her tongue.

8

FAMILY WISDOM

Age/Gray Head

16:31   Gray hair is a crown of glory; it is gained in a righteous life.

17:6   Grandchildren are the crown of the aged, and the glory of children is their fathers.

20:29   The glory of young men is their strength, but the splendor of old men is their gray hair.

Authority/Obedience

1:3   To receive instruction in wise dealing, in righteousness, justice, and equity.

1:5   Let the wise hear and increase in learning, and the one who understands obtain guidance.

1:8   Hear, my son, your father's instruction, and forsake not your mother's teaching.

1:10   My son, if sinners entice you, do not consent.

1:15   My son, do not walk in the way with them; hold back your foot from their paths.

2:1   My son, if you receive my words and treasure up my commandments with you.

2:20   So you will walk in the way of the good and keep to the paths of the righteous.

3:1   My son, do not forget my teaching, but let your heart keep my commandments.

3:21   My son, do not lose sight of these – keep sound wisdom and discretion.

3:26   For the Lord will be your confidence and will keep your foot from being caught.

4:1   Hear, O sons, a father's instruction, and be attentive, that you may gain insight.

4:4   He taught me and said to me, "Let your heart hold fast my words; keep my commandments, and live."

4:6   Do not forsake her, and she will keep you; love her, and she will guard you.

4:10   Hear, my son, and accept my words, that the years of your life may be many.

4:21   Let them not escape from your sight; keep them within your heart.

5:8   Keep your way far from her, and do not go near the door of her house.

6:20   My son, keep your father's commandment, and forsake not your mother's teaching.

6:24   To preserve you from the evil woman, from the smooth tongue of the adulteress.

7:1–2   My son, keep my words and treasure up my commandments with you; keep my commandments and live; keep my teaching as the apple of your eye.

7:5   To keep you from the forbidden woman, from the adulteress with her smooth words.

8:32   And now, O sons, listen to me: blessed are those who keep my ways.

9:6   Leave your simple ways, and live, and walk in the way of insight.

10:8   The wise of heart will receive commandments, but a babbling fool will come to ruin.

13:10   By insolence comes nothing but strife, but with those who take advice is wisdom.

19:16   Whoever keeps the commandments keeps his life; he who despises his ways will die.

22:17–18   Incline your ear, and hear the words of the wise, and apply your heart to my knowledge, for it will be pleasant if you keep them within you, if all of them are ready on your lips.

24:32   Then I saw and considered it; I looked and received instruction.

28:4   Those who forsake the law praise the wicked, but those who keep the law strive against them.

28:7   The one who keeps the law is a son with understanding, but a companion of gluttons shames his father.

28:9   If one turns away his ear from hearing the law, even his prayer is an abomination.

29:18   Where there is no prophetic vision the people cast off restraint, but blessed is he who keeps the law.

Children

1:1–9   The proverbs of Solomon, son of David, king of Israel: To know wisdom and instruction, to understand words of insight, to receive instruction in wise dealing, in righteousness, justice, and equity; to give prudence to the simple, knowledge and discretion to the youth – Let the wise hear and increase in learning, and the one who understands obtain guidance, to understand a proverb and a saying, the words of the wise and their riddles. The fear of the Lord is the beginning of knowledge; fools despise wisdom and instruction. Hear, my son, your father's instruction, and forsake not your mother's teaching, for they are a graceful garland for your head and pendants for your neck.

1:10   My son, if sinners entice you, do not consent.

1:15   My son, do not walk in the way with them; hold back your foot from their paths.

2:1   My son, if you receive my words and treasure up my commandments with you.

3:1–2   My son, do not forget my teaching, but let your heart keep my commandments, for length of days and years of life and peace they will add to you.

3:11–12   My son, do not despise the Lord's discipline or be weary of his reproof, for the Lord reproves him whom he loves, as a father the son in whom he delights.

4:1–4   Hear, O sons, a father's instruction, and be attentive, that you may gain insight, for I give you good precepts; do not forsake my teaching. When I was a son with my father, tender, the only one in the sight of my mother, he taught me and said to me, "Let your heart hold fast my words; keep my commandments, and live."

4:10–13   Hear, my son, and accept my words, that the years of your life may be many. I have taught you the way of wisdom; I have led you in the paths of uprightness. When you walk, your step will not be hampered, and if you run, you will not stumble. Keep hold of instruction; do not let go; guard her, for she is your life.

4:20–21   My son, be attentive to my words; incline your ear to my sayings. Let them not escape from your sight; keep them within your heart.

5:1–2   My son, be attentive to my wisdom; incline your ear to my understanding, that you may keep discretion, and your lips may guard knowledge.

6:1–3   My son, if you have put up security for your neighbor, have given your pledge for a stranger, if you are snared in the words of your mouth, caught in the words of your mouth, then do this, my son, and save yourself, for you have come into the hand of your neighbor: go, hasten, and plead urgently with your neighbor.

6:20–23   My son, keep your father's commandment, and forsake not your mother's teaching. Bind them on your heart always; tie them around your neck. When you walk, they will lead you; when you lie down, they will watch over you; and when you awake, they will talk with you. For the commandment is a lamp and the teaching a light, and the reproofs of discipline are the way of life.

7:1–5   My son, keep my words and treasure up my commandments with you; keep my commandments and live; keep my teaching as the apple of your eye; bind them on your fingers; write them on the tablet of your heart. Say to wisdom, "You are my sister," and call insight your intimate friend, to keep you from the forbidden woman, from the adulteress with her smooth words.

10:1   The proverbs of Solomon. A wise son makes a glad father, but a foolish son is a sorrow to his mother.

10:5   He who gathers in summer is a prudent son, but he who sleeps in harvest is a son who brings shame.

13:1   A wise son hears his father's instruction, but a scoffer does not listen to rebuke.

15:5   A fool despises his father's instruction, but whoever heeds reproof is prudent.

15:20   A wise son makes a glad father, but a foolish man despises his mother.

17:6   Grandchildren are the crown of the aged, and the glory of children is their fathers.

17:21   He who sires a fool gets himself sorrow, and the father of a fool has no joy.

17:25   A foolish son is a grief to his father and bitterness to her who bore him.

19:13   A foolish son is ruin to his father, and a wife's quarreling is a continual dripping of rain.

19:14   House and wealth are inherited from fathers, but a prudent wife is from the Lord.

19:26   He who does violence to his father and chases away his mother is a son who brings shame and reproach.

19:27   Cease to hear instruction, my son, and you will stray from the words of knowledge.

20:20   If one curses his father or his mother, his lamp will be put out in utter darkness.

22:6   Train up a child in the way he should go; even when he is old he will not depart from it.

22:15   Folly is bound up in the heart of a child, but the rod of discipline drives it far from him.

23:13   Do not withhold discipline from a child; if you strike him with a rod, he will not die.

23:22–25   Listen to your father who gave you life, and do not despise your mother when she is old. Buy truth, and do not sell it; buy wisdom, instruction, and understanding. The father of the righteous will greatly rejoice; he who fathers a wise son will be glad in him. Let your father and mother be glad; let her who bore you rejoice.

24:21–22   My son, fear the Lord and the king, and do not join with those who do otherwise, for disaster from them will rise suddenly, and who knows the ruin that will come from them both?

27:11   Be wise, my son, and make my heart glad, that I may answer him who reproaches me.

28:7   The one who keeps the law is a son with understanding, but a companion of gluttons shames his father.

28:24   Whoever robs his father or his mother and says, "That is no transgression," is a companion to a man who destroys.

29:3   He who loves wisdom makes his father glad, but a companion of prostitutes squanders his wealth.

29:15   The rod and reproof give wisdom, but a child left to himself brings shame to his mother.

30:11   There are those who curse their fathers and do not bless their mothers.

30:17   The eye that mocks a father and scorns to obey a mother will be picked out by the ravens of the valley and eaten by the vultures.

31:1–3   The words of King Lemuel. An oracle that his mother taught him: What are you doing, my son? What are you doing, son of my womb? What are you doing, son of my vows? Do not give your strength to women, your ways to those who destroy kings.

31:28   Her children rise up and call her blessed; her husband also, and he praises her.

Correction/Reproof

1:23   If you turn at my reproof, behold, I will pour out my spirit to you; I will make my words known to you.

1:25   Because you have ignored all my counsel and would have none of my reproof.

1:30   Would have none of my counsel and despised all my reproof.

3:11   My son, do not despise the Lord's discipline or be weary of his reproof.

3:12   For the Lord reproves him whom he loves, as a father the son in whom he delights.

5:12   And you say, "How I hated discipline, and my heart despised reproof!"

6:23   For the commandment is a lamp and the teaching a light, and the reproofs of discipline are the way of life.

9:7–9   Whoever corrects a scoffer gets himself abuse, and he who reproves a wicked man incurs injury. Do not reprove a scoffer, or he will hate you; reprove a wise man, and he will love you. Give instruction to a wise man, and he will be still wiser; teach a righteous man, and he will increase in learning.

10:13   On the lips of him who has understanding, wisdom is found, but a rod is for the back of him who lacks sense.

10:17   Whoever heeds instruction is on the path to life, but he who rejects reproof leads others astray.

12:1   Whoever loves discipline loves knowledge, but he who hates reproof is stupid.

13:1   A wise son hears his father's instruction, but a scoffer does not listen to rebuke.

13:18   Poverty and disgrace come to him who ignores instruction, but whoever heeds reproof is honored.

13:24   Whoever spares the rod hates his son, but he who loves him is diligent to discipline him.

14:3   By the mouth of a fool comes a rod for his back, but the lips of the wise will preserve them.

15:5   A fool despises his father's instruction, but whoever heeds reproof is prudent.

15:10   There is severe discipline for him who forsakes the way; whoever hates reproof will die.

15:12   A scoffer does not like to be reproved; he will not go to the wise.

15:31–32   The ear that listens to life-giving reproof will dwell among the wise. Whoever ignores instruction despises himself, but he who listens to reproof gains intelligence.

16:22   Good sense is a fountain of life to him who has it, but the instruction of fools is folly.

17:10   A rebuke goes deeper into a man of understanding than a hundred blows into a fool.

19:18   Discipline your son, for there is hope; do not set your heart on putting him to death.

19:20   Listen to advice and accept instruction, that you may gain wisdom in the future.

19:25   Strike a scoffer, and the simple will learn prudence; reprove a man of understanding, and he will gain knowledge.

19:27   Cease to hear instruction, my son, and you will stray from the words of knowledge.

20:30   Blows that wound cleanse away evil; strokes make clean the innermost parts.

21:11   When a scoffer is punished, the simple becomes wise; when a wise man is instructed, he gains knowledge.

22:15   Folly is bound up in the heart of a child, but the rod of discipline drives it far from him.

23:13–14   Do not withhold discipline from a child; if you strike him with a rod, he will not die. If you strike him with the rod, you will save his soul from Sheol.

24:25   But those who rebuke the wicked will have delight, and a good blessing will come upon them.

25:12   Like a gold ring or an ornament of gold is a wise reprover to a listening ear.

26:3   A whip for the horse, a bridle for the donkey, and a rod for the back of fools.

27:5   Better is open rebuke than hidden love.

28:23   Whoever rebukes a man will afterward find more favor than he who flatters with his tongue.

29:1   He who is often reproved, yet stiffens his neck, will suddenly be broken beyond healing.

29:15   The rod and reproof give wisdom, but a child left to himself brings shame to his mother.

29:17   Discipline your son, and he will give you rest; he will give delight to your heart.

30:6   Do not add to his words, lest he rebuke you and you be found a liar.

Descendants

11:21   Be assured, an evil person will not go unpunished, but the offspring of the righteous will be delivered.

13:22   A good man leaves an inheritance to his children's children, but the sinner's wealth is laid up for the righteous.

14:26   In the fear of the Lord one has strong confidence, and his children will have a refuge.

20:7   The righteous who walks in his integrity – blessed are his children after him!

31:28   Her children rise up and call her blessed; her husband also, and he praises her.

Discipline/Training

1:23   If you turn at my reproof, behold, I will pour out my spirit to you; I will make my words known to you.

3:11–12   My son, do not despise the Lord's discipline or be weary of his reproof, for the Lord reproves him whom he loves, as a father the son in whom he delights.

6:23   For the commandment is a lamp and the teaching a light, and the reproofs of discipline are the way of life.

9:8   Do not reprove a scoffer, or he will hate you; reprove a wise man, and he will love you.

10:17   Whoever heeds instruction is on the path to life, but he who rejects reproof leads others astray.

12:1 Whoever loves discipline loves knowledge, but he who hates reproof is stupid.

13:1 A wise son hears his father's instruction, but a scoffer does not listen to rebuke.

13:18 Poverty and disgrace come to him who ignores instruction, but whoever heeds reproof is honored.

13:24 Whoever spares the rod hates his son, but he who loves him is diligent to discipline him.

15:5 A fool despises his father's instruction, but whoever heeds reproof is prudent.

15:10 There is severe discipline for him who forsakes the way; whoever hates reproof will die.

15:12 A scoffer does not like to be reproved; he will not go to the wise.

15:31–32 The ear that listens to life-giving reproof will dwell among the wise. Whoever ignores instruction despises himself, but he who listens to reproof gains intelligence.

16:22 Good sense is a fountain of life to him who has it, but the instruction of fools is folly.

19:18 Discipline your son, for there is hope; do not set your heart on putting him to death.

19:20 Listen to advice and accept instruction, that you may gain wisdom in the future.

19:25 Strike a scoffer, and the simple will learn prudence; reprove a man of understanding, and he will gain knowledge.

19:27 Cease to hear instruction, my son, and you will stray from the words of knowledge.

20:30 Blows that wound cleanse away evil; strokes make clean the innermost parts.

22:6 Train up a child in the way he should go; even when he is old he will not depart from it.

22:15 Folly is bound up in the heart of a child, but the rod of discipline drives it far from him.

23:12–14 Apply your heart to instruction and your ear to words of knowledge. Do not withhold discipline from a child; if you strike him with a rod, he will not die. If you strike him with the rod, you will save his soul from Sheol.

25:12   Like a gold ring or an ornament of gold is a wise reprover to a listening ear.

29:15   The rod and reproof give wisdom, but a child left to himself brings shame to his mother.

Marriage

2:17   Who forsakes the companion of her youth and forgets the covenant of her God.

5:15–19   Drink water from your own cistern, flowing water from your own well. Should your springs be scattered abroad, streams of water in the streets? Let them be for yourself alone, and not for strangers with you. Let your fountain be blessed, and rejoice in the wife of your youth, a lovely deer, a graceful doe. Let her breasts fill you at all times with delight; be intoxicated always in her love.

6:29   So is he who goes in to his neighbor's wife; none who touches her will go unpunished.

11:16   A gracious woman gets honor, and violent men get riches.

12:4   An excellent wife is the crown of her husband, but she who brings shame is like rottenness in his bones.

14:1   The wisest of women builds her house, but folly with her own hands tears it down.

18:22   He who finds a wife finds a good thing and obtains favor from the Lord.

19:13–14   A foolish son is ruin to his father, and a wife's quarreling is a continual dripping of rain. House and wealth are inherited from fathers, but a prudent wife is from the Lord.

21:9   It is better to live in a corner of the housetop than in a house shared with a quarrelsome wife.

21:19   It is better to live in a desert land than with a quarrelsome and fretful woman.

24:3–4   By wisdom a house is built, and by understanding it is established; by knowledge the rooms are filled with all precious and pleasant riches.

25:24   It is better to live in a corner of the housetop than in a house shared with a quarrelsome wife.

27:8   Like a bird that strays from its nest is a man who strays from his home.

27:15–16   A continual dripping on a rainy day and a quarrelsome wife are alike; to restrain her is to restrain the wind or to grasp oil in one's right hand.

31:10–29   An excellent wife who can find? She is far more precious than jewels. The heart of her husband trusts in her, and he will have no lack of gain. She does him good, and not harm, all the days of her life. She seeks wool and flax, and works with willing hands. She is like the ships of the merchant; she brings her food from afar. She rises while it is yet night and provides food for her household and portions for her maidens. She considers a field and buys it; with the fruit of her hands she plants a vineyard. She dresses herself with strength and makes her arms strong. She perceives that her merchandise is profitable. Her lamp does not go out at night. She puts her hands to the distaff, and her hands hold the spindle. She opens her hand to the poor and reaches out her hands to the needy. She is not afraid of snow for her household, for all her household are clothed in scarlet. She makes bed coverings for herself; her clothing is fine linen and purple. Her husband is known in the gates when he sits among the elders of the land. She makes linen garments and sells them; she delivers sashes to the merchant. Strength and dignity are her clothing, and she laughs at the time to come. She opens her mouth with wisdom, and the teaching of kindness is on her tongue. She looks well to the ways of her household and does not eat the bread of idleness. Her children rise up and call her blessed; her husband also, and he praises her: Many women have done excellently, but you surpass them all.

Parents

1:1–9   The proverbs of Solomon, son of David, king of Israel: To know wisdom and instruction, to understand words of insight, to receive instruction in wise dealing, in righteousness, justice, and equity; to give prudence to the simple, knowledge and discretion to the youth – Let the wise hear and increase in learning, and the one who understands obtain guidance, to understand a proverb and a saying, the words of the wise and their riddles. The fear of the Lord is the beginning of knowledge; fools despise wisdom and instruction. Hear, my son, your father's instruction, and forsake not your mother's teaching, for they are a graceful garland for your head and pendants for your neck.

1:10   My son, if sinners entice you, do not consent.

1:15   My son, do not walk in the way with them; hold back your foot from their paths.

2:1   My son, if you receive my words and treasure up my commandments with you.

3:1–2   My son, do not forget my teaching, but let your heart keep my commandments, for length of days and years of life and peace they will add to you.

3:11–12   My son, do not despise the Lord's discipline or be weary of his reproof, for the Lord reproves him whom he loves, as a father the son in whom he delights.

3:21   My son, do not lose sight of these – keep sound wisdom and discretion.

4:1–4   Hear, O sons, a father's instruction, and be attentive, that you may gain insight, for I give you good precepts; do not forsake my teaching. When I was a son with my father, tender, the only one in the sight of my mother, he taught me and said to me, "Let your heart hold fast my words; keep my commandments, and live."

4:10–13   Hear, my son, and accept my words, that the years of your life may be many. I have taught you the way of wisdom; I have led you in the paths of uprightness. When you walk, your step will not be hampered, and if you run, you will not stumble. Keep hold of instruction; do not let go; guard her, for she is your life.

4:20–21   My son, be attentive to my words; incline your ear to my sayings. Let them not escape from your sight; keep them within your heart.

5:1–2   My son, be attentive to my wisdom; incline your ear to my understanding, that you may keep discretion, and your lips may guard knowledge.

5:20   Why should you be intoxicated, my son, with a forbidden woman and embrace the bosom of an adulteress?

6:1–3   My son, if you have put up security for your neighbor, have given your pledge for a stranger, if you are snared in the words of your mouth, caught in the words of your mouth, then do this, my son, and save yourself, for you have come into the hand of your neighbor: go, hasten, and plead urgently with your neighbor.

6:20–23   My son, keep your father's commandment, and forsake not your mother's teaching. Bind them on your heart always; tie them around your neck. When you walk, they will lead you; when you lie down, they will watch over you; and when you awake, they will talk with you. For the commandment is a lamp and the teaching a light, and the reproofs of discipline are the way of life.

7:1–5   My son, keep my words and treasure up my commandments with you; keep my commandments and live; keep my teaching as the apple of your eye; bind them on your fingers; write them on the tablet of your heart. Say to wisdom, "You are my sister," and call insight your intimate friend, to keep you from the forbidden woman, from the adulteress with her smooth words.

10:1   The proverbs of Solomon. A wise son makes a glad father, but a foolish son is a sorrow to his mother.

10:5   He who gathers in summer is a prudent son, but he who sleeps in harvest is a son who brings shame.

11:29   Whoever troubles his own household will inherit the wind, and the fool will be servant to the wise of heart.

13:1   A wise son hears his father's instruction, but a scoffer does not listen to rebuke.

13:22   A good man leaves an inheritance to his children's children, but the sinner's wealth is laid up for the righteous.

13:24   Whoever spares the rod hates his son, but he who loves him is diligent to discipline him.

14:1   The wisest of women builds her house, but folly with her own hands tears it down.

14:26   In the fear of the Lord one has strong confidence, and his children will have a refuge.

15:20   A wise son makes a glad father, but a foolish man despises his mother.

17:2   A servant who deals wisely will rule over a son who acts shamefully and will share the inheritance as one of the brothers.

17:6   Grandchildren are the crown of the aged, and the glory of children is their fathers.

17:21   He who sires a fool gets himself sorrow, and the father of a fool has no joy.

17:25   A foolish son is a grief to his father and bitterness to her who bore him.

19:13–14   A foolish son is ruin to his father, and a wife's quarreling is a continual dripping of rain. House and wealth are inherited from fathers, but a prudent wife is from the Lord.

19:18   Discipline your son, for there is hope; do not set your heart on putting him to death.

19:26–27   He who does violence to his father and chases away his mother is a son who brings shame and reproach. Cease to hear instruction, my son, and you will stray from the words of knowledge.

20:7   The righteous who walks in his integrity – blessed are his children after him!

20:20   If one curses his father or his mother, his lamp will be put out in utter darkness.

22:6   Train up a child in the way he should go; even when he is old he will not depart from it.

22:15   Folly is bound up in the heart of a child, but the rod of discipline drives it far from him.

23:13–16   Do not withhold discipline from a child; if you strike him with a rod, he will not die. If you strike him with the rod, you will save his soul from Sheol. My son, if your heart is wise, my heart too will be glad. My inmost being will exult when your lips speak what is right.

23:19   Hear, my son, and be wise, and direct your heart in the way.

23:22   Listen to your father who gave you life, and do not despise your mother when she is old.

23:24–25   The father of the righteous will greatly rejoice; he who fathers a wise son will be glad in him. Let your father and mother be glad; let her who bore you rejoice.

24:13   My son, eat honey, for it is good, and the drippings of the honeycomb are sweet to your taste.

24:21–22   My son, fear the Lord and the king, and do not join with those who do otherwise, for disaster from them will rise suddenly, and who knows the ruin that will come from them both?

27:11   Be wise, my son, and make my heart glad, that I may answer him who reproaches me.

28:7   The one who keeps the law is a son with understanding, but a companion of gluttons shames his father.

28:24   Whoever robs his father or his mother and says, "That is no transgression," is a companion to a man who destroys.

29:3   He who loves wisdom makes his father glad, but a companion of prostitutes squanders his wealth.

29:15   The rod and reproof give wisdom, but a child left to himself brings shame to his mother.

29:17   Discipline your son, and he will give you rest; he will give delight to your heart.

30:11   There are those who curse their fathers and do not bless their mothers.

30:17   The eye that mocks a father and scorns to obey a mother will be picked out by the ravens of the valley and eaten by the vultures.

31:1   The words of King Lemuel. An oracle that his mother taught him.

31:10–29   An excellent wife who can find? She is far more precious than jewels. The heart of her husband trusts in her, and he will have no lack of gain. She does him good, and not harm, all the days of her life. She seeks wool and flax, and works with willing hands. She is like the ships of the merchant; she brings her food from afar. She rises while it is yet night and provides food for her household and portions for her maidens. She considers a field and buys it; with the fruit of her hands she plants a vineyard. She dresses herself with strength and makes her arms strong. She perceives that her merchandise is profitable. Her lamp does not go out at night. She puts her hands to the distaff, and her hands hold the spindle. She opens her hand to the poor and reaches out her hands to the needy. She is not afraid of snow for her household, for all her household are clothed in scarlet. She makes bed coverings for herself; her clothing is fine linen and purple. Her husband is known in the gates when he sits among the elders of the land. She makes linen garments and sells them; she delivers sashes to the merchant. Strength and dignity are her clothing, and she laughs at the time to come. She opens her mouth with wisdom, and the teaching of kindness is on her tongue. She looks well to the ways of her household and does not eat the bread of idleness. Her children rise up and call her blessed; her husband also, and he praises her: Many women have done excellently, but you surpass them all.

9

INTELLECTUAL WISDOM

Wisdom/Understanding/Knowledge

Wisdom

1:1–7   The proverbs of Solomon, son of David, king of Israel: To know wisdom and instruction, to understand words of insight, to receive instruction in wise dealing, in righteousness, justice, and equity; to give prudence to the simple, knowledge and discretion to the youth – Let the wise hear and increase in learning, and the one who understands obtain guidance, to understand a proverb and a saying, the words of the wise and their riddles. The fear of the Lord is the beginning of knowledge; fools despise wisdom and instruction.

1:20–33   Wisdom cries aloud in the street, in the markets she raises her voice; at the head of the noisy streets she cries out; at the entrance of the city gates she speaks: "How long, O simple ones, will you love being simple? How long will scoffers delight in their scoffing and fools hate knowledge? If you turn at my reproof, behold, I will pour out my spirit to you; I will make my words known to you. Because I have called and you refused to listen, have stretched out my hand and no one has heeded, because you have ignored all my counsel and would have none of my reproof, I also will laugh at your calamity; I will mock when terror strikes you, when terror strikes you like a storm and your calamity comes like a whirlwind, when distress and anguish come upon you. Then they will call upon me, but I will not answer; they will seek me diligently but will not find me. Because they hated knowledge and did not choose the fear of the Lord, would have none of my counsel and despised all my reproof, therefore they shall eat the fruit of their way, and have their fill of their own devices. For the simple are killed by their turning away, and the complacency of fools destroys them; but whoever listens to me will dwell secure and will be at ease, without dread of disaster."

2:1–10 My son, if you receive my words and treasure up my commandments with you, making your ear attentive to wisdom and inclining your heart to understanding; yes, if you call out for insight and raise your voice for understanding, if you seek it like silver and search for it as for hidden treasures, then you will understand the fear of the Lord and find the knowledge of God. For the Lord gives wisdom; from his mouth come knowledge and understanding; he stores up sound wisdom for the upright; he is a shield to those who walk in integrity, guarding the paths of justice and watching over the way of his saints. Then you will understand righteousness and justice and equity, every good path; for wisdom will come into your heart, and knowledge will be pleasant to your soul.

3:7 Be not wise in your own eyes; fear the Lord, and turn away from evil.

3:13–26 Blessed is the one who finds wisdom, and the one who gets understanding, for the gain from her is better than gain from silver and her profit better than gold. She is more precious than jewels, and nothing you desire can compare with her. Long life is in her right hand; in her left hand are riches and honor. Her ways are ways of pleasantness, and all her paths are peace. She is a tree of life to those who lay hold of her; those who hold her fast are called blessed. The Lord by wisdom founded the earth; by understanding he established the heavens; by his knowledge the deeps broke open, and the clouds drop down the dew. My son, do not lose sight of these – keep sound wisdom and discretion, and they will be life for your soul and adornment for your neck. Then you will walk on your way securely, and your foot will not stumble. If you lie down, you will not be afraid; when you lie down, your sleep will be sweet.

Do not be afraid of sudden terror or of the ruin of the wicked, when it comes, for the Lord will be your confidence and will keep your foot from being caught.

3:35   The wise will inherit honor, but fools get disgrace.

4:5–9   Get wisdom; get insight; do not forget, and do not turn away from the words of my mouth. Do not forsake her, and she will keep you; love her, and she will guard you. The beginning of wisdom is this: Get wisdom, and whatever you get, get insight. Prize her highly, and she will exalt you; she will honor you if you embrace her. She will place on your head a graceful garland; she will bestow on you a beautiful crown.

4:11   I have taught you the way of wisdom; I have led you in the paths of uprightness.

5:1   My son, be attentive to my wisdom; incline your ear to my understanding.

6:6   Go to the ant, O sluggard; consider her ways, and be wise.

7:4   Say to wisdom, "You are my sister," and call insight your intimate friend.

8:1–36   Does not wisdom call? Does not understanding raise her voice? On the heights beside the way, at the crossroads she takes her stand; beside the gates in front of the town, at the entrance of the portals she cries aloud: "To you, O men, I call, and my cry is to the children of man. O simple ones, learn prudence; O fools, learn sense. Hear, for I will speak noble things, and from my lips will come what is right, for my mouth will utter truth; wickedness is an abomination to my lips. All the words of my mouth are righteous; there is nothing twisted or crooked in them. They are all straight to him who understands, and right to those who find knowledge. Take my instruction instead of silver, and knowledge rather than choice gold, for wisdom is better than jewels, and all that you may desire cannot compare with her. I, wisdom, dwell with prudence, and I find knowledge and discretion. The fear of the Lord is hatred of evil. Pride and arrogance and the way of evil and perverted speech I hate. I have counsel and sound wisdom; I have insight; I have strength. By me kings reign, and rulers decree what is just; by me princes rule, and nobles, all who govern justly. I love those who love me, and those who seek me diligently find me. Riches and honor are with me, enduring wealth and righteousness. My fruit is better than gold, even fine gold, and my yield than choice silver. I walk in the way of righteousness, in the paths of justice, granting an inheritance to those who love me, and filling their treasuries. The Lord possessed me at the beginning of his work, the first of his acts of old. Ages ago I was set up, at the first, before the beginning of the earth. When there were no depths I was brought forth, when there were no springs abounding with water. Before the mountains had been shaped, before the hills, I was brought forth, before he had made the earth with its fields, or the first of the dust of the world. When he established the heavens, I was there; when he drew a circle on the face of the deep, when he made firm the skies above, when he established the fountains of the deep, when he assigned to the sea its limit, so that the waters might not transgress his command, when he marked out the foundations of the earth, then I was beside him, like a master workman, and I was daily his delight, rejoicing before him always, rejoicing in his inhabited world and delighting in the children of man. And now, O sons, listen to me: blessed are those who keep my ways. Hear instruction and be wise, and do not neglect it. Blessed is the one who listens to me, watching daily at my gates, waiting beside my doors. For whoever finds me finds life and obtains favor from the Lord, but he who fails to find me injures himself; all who hate me love death."

9:1–12 Wisdom has built her house; she has hewn her seven pillars. She has slaughtered her beasts; she has mixed her wine; she has also set her table. She has sent out her young women to call from the highest places in the town, "Whoever is simple, let him turn in here!" To him who lacks sense she says, "Come, eat of my bread and drink of the wine I have mixed. Leave your simple ways, and live, and walk in the way of insight." Whoever corrects a scoffer gets himself abuse, and he who reproves a wicked man incurs injury. Do not reprove a scoffer, or he will hate you; reprove a wise man, and he will love you. Give instruction to a wise man, and he will be still wiser; teach a righteous man, and he will increase in learning. The fear of the Lord is the beginning of wisdom, and the knowledge of the Holy One is insight. For by me your days will be multiplied, and years will be added to your life. If you are wise, you are wise for yourself; if you scoff, you alone will bear it.

10:1 The proverbs of Solomon. A wise son makes a glad father, but a foolish son is a sorrow to his mother.

10:5 He who gathers in summer is a prudent son, but he who sleeps in harvest is a son who brings shame.

10:8 The wise of heart will receive commandments, but a babbling fool will come to ruin.

10:13–14 On the lips of him who has understanding, wisdom is found, but a rod is for the back of him who lacks sense. The wise lay up knowledge, but the mouth of a fool brings ruin near.

10:19 When words are many, transgression is not lacking, but whoever restrains his lips is prudent.

10:23 Doing wrong is like a joke to a fool, but wisdom is pleasure to a man of understanding.

10:31 The mouth of the righteous brings forth wisdom, but the perverse tongue will be cut off.

11:2 When pride comes, then comes disgrace, but with the humble is wisdom.

11:29–30 Whoever troubles his own household will inherit the wind, and the fool will be servant to the wise of heart. The fruit of the righteous is a tree of life, and whoever captures souls is wise.

12:15–16 The way of a fool is right in his own eyes, but a wise man listens to advice. The vexation of a fool is known at once, but the prudent ignores an insult.

12:18 There is one whose rash words are like sword thrusts, but the tongue of the wise brings healing.

12:23 A prudent man conceals knowledge, but the heart of fools proclaims folly.

13:1 A wise son hears his father's instruction, but a scoffer does not listen to rebuke.

13:10 By insolence comes nothing but strife, but with those who take advice is wisdom.

13:14 The teaching of the wise is a fountain of life, that one may turn away from the snares of death.

13:20 Whoever walks with the wise becomes wise, but the companion of fools will suffer harm.

14:1 The wisest of women builds her house, but folly with her own hands tears it down.

14:3 By the mouth of a fool comes a rod for his back, but the lips of the wise will preserve them.

14:6 A scoffer seeks wisdom in vain, but knowledge is easy for a man of understanding.

14:8 The wisdom of the prudent is to discern his way, but the folly of fools is deceiving.

14:16 One who is wise is cautious and turns away from evil, but a fool is reckless and careless.

14:24 The crown of the wise is their wealth, but the folly of fools brings folly.

14:33 Wisdom rests in the heart of a man of understanding, but it makes itself known even in the midst of fools.

14:35 A servant who deals wisely has the king's favor, but his wrath falls on one who acts shamefully.

15:2 The tongue of the wise commends knowledge, but the mouths of fools pour out folly.

15:5 A fool despises his father's instruction, but whoever heeds reproof is prudent.

15:7 The lips of the wise spread knowledge; not so the hearts of fools.

15:12 A scoffer does not like to be reproved; he will not go to the wise.

15:20 A wise son makes a glad father, but a foolish man despises his mother.

15:24 The path of life leads upward for the prudent, that he may turn away from Sheol beneath.

15:31–33   The ear that listens to life-giving reproof will dwell among the wise. Whoever ignores instruction despises himself, but he who listens to reproof gains intelligence. The fear of the Lord is instruction in wisdom, and humility comes before honor.

16:14   A king's wrath is a messenger of death, and a wise man will appease it.

16:16   How much better to get wisdom than gold! To get understanding is to be chosen rather than silver.

16:21   The wise of heart is called discerning, and sweetness of speech increases persuasiveness.

16:23   The heart of the wise makes his speech judicious and adds persuasiveness to his lips.

17:2   A servant who deals wisely will rule over a son who acts shamefully and will share the inheritance as one of the brothers.

17:24   The discerning sets his face toward wisdom, but the eyes of a fool are on the ends of the earth.

17:28   Even a fool who keeps silent is considered wise; when he closes his lips, he is deemed intelligent.

18:1   Whoever isolates himself seeks his own desire; he breaks out against all sound judgment.

18:4   The words of a man's mouth are deep waters; the fountain of wisdom is a bubbling brook.

18:15   An intelligent heart acquires knowledge, and the ear of the wise seeks knowledge.

19:8   Whoever gets sense loves his own soul; he who keeps understanding will discover good.

19:20   Listen to advice and accept instruction, that you may gain wisdom in the future.

20:1   Wine is a mocker, strong drink a brawler, and whoever is led astray by it is not wise.

20:18   Plans are established by counsel; by wise guidance wage war.

20:26   A wise king winnows the wicked and drives the wheel over them.

21:11   When a scoffer is punished, the simple becomes wise; when a wise man is instructed, he gains knowledge.

21:20   Precious treasure and oil are in a wise man's dwelling, but a foolish man devours it.

21:22   A wise man scales the city of the mighty and brings down the stronghold in which they trust.

21:30   No wisdom, no understanding, no counsel can avail against the Lord.

22:3   The prudent sees danger and hides himself, but the simple go on and suffer for it.

22:17–21   Incline your ear, and hear the words of the wise, and apply your heart to 33knowledge, for it will be pleasant if you keep them within you, if all of them are ready on your lips. That your trust may be in the Lord, I have made them known to you today, even to you. Have I not written for you thirty sayings of counsel and knowledge, to make you know what is right and true, that you may give a true answer to those who sent you?

23:9   Do not speak in the hearing of a fool, for he will despise the good sense of your words.

23:15–16   My son, if your heart is wise, my heart too will be glad. My inmost being will exult when your lips speak what is right.

23:19   Hear, my son, and be wise, and direct your heart in the way.

23:22–24   Listen to your father who gave you life, and do not despise your mother when she is old. Buy truth, and do not sell it; buy wisdom, instruction, and understanding. The father of the righteous will greatly rejoice; he who fathers a wise son will be glad in him.

24:3–7   By wisdom a house is built, and by understanding it is established; by knowledge the rooms are filled with all precious and pleasant riches. A wise man is full of strength, and a man of knowledge enhances his might, for by wise guidance you can wage your war, and in abundance of counselors there is victory. Wisdom is too high for a fool; in the gate he does not open his mouth.

24:13–14   My son, eat honey, for it is good, and the drippings of the honeycomb are sweet to your taste. Know that wisdom is such to your soul; if you find it, there will be a future, and your hope will not be cut off.

24:23   These also are sayings of the wise. Partiality in judging is not good.

25:12   Like a gold ring or an ornament of gold is a wise reprover to a listening ear.

26:5   Answer a fool according to his folly, lest he be wise in his own eyes.

26:12   Do you see a man who is wise in his own eyes? There is more hope for a fool than for him.

26:16   The sluggard is wiser in his own eyes than seven men who can answer sensibly.

27:11–12   Be wise, my son, and make my heart glad, that I may answer him who reproaches me. The prudent sees danger and hides himself, but the simple go on and suffer for it.

28:11   A rich man is wise in his own eyes, but a poor man who has understanding will find him out.

28:26   Whoever trusts in his own mind is a fool, but he who walks in wisdom will be delivered.

29:3   He who loves wisdom makes his father glad, but a companion of prostitutes squanders his wealth.

29:8   Scoffers set a city aflame, but the wise turn away wrath.

29:9   If a wise man has an argument with a fool, the fool only rages and laughs, and there is no quiet.

29:11   A fool gives full vent to his spirit, but a wise man quietly holds it back.

29:15   The rod and reproof give wisdom, but a child left to himself brings shame to his mother.

30:24–28   Four things on earth are small, but they are exceedingly wise: the ants are a people not strong, yet they provide their food in the summer; the rock badgers are a people not mighty, yet they make their homes in the cliffs; the locusts have no king, yet all of them march in rank; the lizard you can take in your hands, yet it is in kings' palaces.

31:26　She opens her mouth with wisdom, and the teaching of kindness is on her tongue.

Understanding

1:2　To know wisdom and instruction, to understand words of insight.

1:5　Let the wise hear and increase in learning, and the one who understands obtain guidance.

1:6　To understand a proverb and a saying, the words of the wise and their riddles.

2:1–22　My son, if you receive my words and treasure up my commandments with you, making your ear attentive to wisdom and inclining your heart to understanding; yes, if you call out for insight and raise your voice for understanding, if you seek it like silver and search for it as for hidden treasures, then you will understand the fear of the Lord and find the knowledge of God. For the Lord gives wisdom; from his mouth come knowledge and understanding; he stores up sound wisdom for the upright; he is a shield to those who walk in integrity, guarding the paths of justice and watching over the way of his saints. Then you will understand righteousness and justice and equity, every good path; for wisdom will come into your heart, and knowledge will be pleasant to your soul; discretion will watch over you, understanding will guard you, delivering you from the way of evil, from men of perverted speech, who forsake the paths of uprightness to walk in the ways of darkness, who rejoice in doing evil and delight in the perverseness of evil, men whose paths are crooked, and who are devious in their ways. So you will be delivered from the forbidden woman, from the adulteress with her smooth words, who forsakes the companion of her youth and forgets the covenant of her God; for her house sinks down to death, and her paths to the departed; none who go to her come back, nor do they regain the paths of life. So you will walk in the way of the good and keep to the paths of the righteous. For the upright will inhabit the land, and those with integrity will remain in it, but the wicked will be cut off from the land, and the treacherous will be rooted out of it.

3:5–6   Trust in the Lord with all your heart, and do not lean on your own understanding. In all your ways acknowledge him, and he will make straight your paths.

3:13   Blessed is the one who finds wisdom, and the one who gets understanding.

3:19   The Lord by wisdom founded the earth; by understanding he established the heavens.

4:1   Hear, O sons, a father's instruction, and be attentive, that you may gain insight.

4:5   Get wisdom; get insight; do not forget, and do not turn away from the words of my mouth.

4:7   The beginning of wisdom is this: Get wisdom, and whatever you get, get insight.

5:1   My son, be attentive to my wisdom; incline your ear to my understanding.

7:4   Say to wisdom, "You are my sister," and call insight your intimate friend.

8:1   Does not wisdom call? Does not understanding raise her voice?

8:9   They are all straight to him who understands, and right to those who find knowledge.

8:14   I have counsel and sound wisdom; I have insight; I have strength.

9:4   "Whoever is simple, let him turn in here!"

9:6   Leave your simple ways, and live, and walk in the way of insight.

9:10   The fear of the Lord is the beginning of wisdom, and the knowledge of the Holy One is insight.

9:16   "Whoever is simple, let him turn in here!"

10:13   On the lips of him who has understanding, wisdom is found, but a rod is for the back of him who lacks sense.

10:21   The lips of the righteous feed many, but fools die for lack of sense.

10:23   Doing wrong is like a joke to a fool, but wisdom is pleasure to a man of understanding.

11:12   Whoever belittles his neighbor lacks sense, but a man of understanding remains silent.

12:8   A man is commended according to his good sense, but one of twisted mind is despised.

13:15   Good sense wins favor, but the way of the treacherous is their ruin.

14:6   A scoffer seeks wisdom in vain, but knowledge is easy for a man of understanding.

14:8   The wisdom of the prudent is to discern his way, but the folly of fools is deceiving.

14:29   Whoever is slow to anger has great understanding, but he who has a hasty temper exalts folly.

14:33   Wisdom rests in the heart of a man of understanding, but it makes itself known even in the midst of fools.

15:14   The heart of him who has understanding seeks knowledge, but the mouths of fools feed on folly.

15:21   Folly is a joy to him who lacks sense, but a man of understanding walks straight ahead.

15:32   Whoever ignores instruction despises himself, but he who listens to reproof gains intelligence.

16:16   How much better to get wisdom than gold! To get understanding is to be chosen rather than silver.

16:22   Good sense is a fountain of life to him who has it, but the instruction of fools is folly.

17:10   A rebuke goes deeper into a man of understanding than a hundred blows into a fool.

17:24   The discerning sets his face toward wisdom, but the eyes of a fool are on the ends of the earth.

17:27   Whoever restrains his words has knowledge, and he who has a cool spirit is a man of understanding.

18:2   A fool takes no pleasure in understanding, but only in expressing his opinion.

19:8   Whoever gets sense loves his own soul; he who keeps understanding will discover good.

19:25   Strike a scoffer, and the simple will learn prudence; reprove a man of understanding, and he will gain knowledge.

20:5   The purpose in a man's heart is like deep water, but a man of understanding will draw it out.

20:24   A man's steps are from the Lord, how then can man understand his way?

21:16   One who wanders from the way of good sense will rest in the assembly of the dead.

21:30   No wisdom, no understanding, no counsel can avail against the Lord.

23:22–23   Listen to your father who gave you life, and do not despise your mother when she is old. Buy truth, and do not sell it; buy wisdom, instruction, and understanding.

24:3–4   By wisdom a house is built, and by understanding it is established; by knowledge the rooms are filled with all precious and pleasant riches.

28:2   When a land transgresses, it has many rulers, but with a man of understanding and knowledge, its stability will long continue.

28:5   Evil men do not understand justice, but those who seek the Lord understand it completely.

28:11   A rich man is wise in his own eyes, but a poor man who has understanding will find him out.

28:16   A ruler who lacks understanding is a cruel oppressor, but he who hates unjust gain will prolong his days.

29:7   A righteous man knows the rights of the poor; a wicked man does not understand such knowledge.

30:18–19   Three things are too wonderful for me; four I do not understand: the way of an eagle in the sky, the way of a serpent on a rock, the way of a ship on the high seas, and the way of a man with a virgin.

Knowledge

1:2   To know wisdom and instruction, to understand words of insight.

1:4   To give prudence to the simple, knowledge and discretion to the youth.

1:7   The fear of the Lord is the beginning of knowledge; fools despise wisdom and instruction.

1:22   How long, O simple ones, will you love being simple? How long will scoffers delight in their scoffing and fools hate knowledge?

1:29   Because they hated knowledge and did not choose the fear of the Lord.

2:5–6   Then you will understand the fear of the Lord and find the knowledge of God. For the Lord gives wisdom; from his mouth come knowledge and understanding.

2:10   For wisdom will come into your heart, and knowledge will be pleasant to your soul.

3:20   By his knowledge the deeps broke open, and the clouds drop down the dew.

4:19   The way of the wicked is like deep darkness; they do not know over what they stumble.

5:2   That you may keep discretion, and your lips may guard knowledge.

5:6   She does not ponder the path of life; her ways wander, and she does not know it.

7:23   As a bird rushes into a snare; he does not know that it will cost him his life.

8:9–10   They are all straight to him who understands, and right to those who find knowledge. Take my instruction instead of silver, and knowledge rather than choice gold.

8:12   I, wisdom, dwell with prudence, and I find knowledge and discretion.

9:10   The fear of the Lord is the beginning of wisdom, and the knowledge of the Holy One is insight.

9:18   But he does not know that the dead are there, that her guests are in the depths of Sheol.

10:14   The wise lay up knowledge, but the mouth of a fool brings ruin near.

11:9   With his mouth the godless man would destroy his neighbor, but by knowledge the righteous are delivered.

12:1   Whoever loves discipline loves knowledge, but he who hates reproof is stupid.

12:23   A prudent man conceals knowledge, but the heart of fools proclaims folly.

13:16   In everything the prudent acts with knowledge, but a fool flaunts his folly.

14:6–7   A scoffer seeks wisdom in vain, but knowledge is easy for a man of understanding. Leave the presence of a fool, for there you do not meet words of knowledge.

14:18   The simple inherit folly, but the prudent are crowned with knowledge.

15:2   The tongue of the wise commends knowledge, but the mouths of fools pour out folly.

15:7   The lips of the wise spread knowledge; not so the hearts of fools.

15:14   The heart of him who has understanding seeks knowledge, but the mouths of fools feed on folly.

17:27   Whoever restrains his words has knowledge, and he who has a cool spirit is a man of understanding.

18:15   An intelligent heart acquires knowledge, and the ear of the wise seeks knowledge.

19:2   Desire without knowledge is not good, and whoever makes haste with his feet misses his way.

19:25   Strike a scoffer, and the simple will learn prudence; reprove a man of understanding, and he will gain knowledge.

19:27   Cease to hear instruction, my son, and you will stray from the words of knowledge.

20:15   There is gold and abundance of costly stones, but the lips of knowledge are a precious jewel.

21:11 When a scoffer is punished, the simple becomes wise; when a wise man is instructed, he gains knowledge.

22:12 The eyes of the Lord keep watch over knowledge, but he overthrows the words of the traitor.

22:17–21 Incline your ear, and hear the words of the wise, and apply your heart to my knowledge, for it will be pleasant if you keep them within you, if all of them are ready on your lips. That your trust may be in the Lord, I have made them known to you today, even to you. Have I not written for you thirty sayings of counsel and knowledge, to make you know what is right and true, that you may give a true answer to those who sent you?

23:10–12 Do not move an ancient landmark or enter the fields of the fatherless, for their Redeemer is strong; he will plead their cause against you. Apply your heart to instruction and your ear to words of knowledge.

24:3–5 By wisdom a house is built, and by understanding it is established; by knowledge the rooms are filled with all precious and pleasant riches. A wise man is full of strength, and a man of knowledge enhances his might.

24:12 If you say, "Behold, we did not know this," does not he who weighs the heart perceive it? Does not he who keeps watch over your soul know it, and will he not repay man according to his work?

24:14 Know that wisdom is such to your soul; if you find it, there will be a future, and your hope will not be cut off.

27:1 Do not boast about tomorrow, for you do not know what a day may bring.

27:23 Know well the condition of your flocks, and give attention to your herds.

28:2 When a land transgresses, it has many rulers, but with a man of understanding and knowledge, its stability will long continue.

28:22 A stingy man hastens after wealth and does not know that poverty will come upon him.

30:1–4 The words of Agur son of Jakeh. The oracle. The man declares, I am weary, O God; I am weary, O God, and worn out.

Surely I am too stupid to be a man. I have not the understanding of a man. I have not learned wisdom, nor have I knowledge of the Holy One. Who has ascended to heaven and come down? Who has gathered the wind in his fists? Who has wrapped up the waters in a garment? Who has established all the ends of the earth? What is his name, and what is his son's name? Surely you know!

10

MARKETPLACE WISDOM

Integrity/Dishonesty

2:7 He stores up sound wisdom for the upright; he is a shield to those who walk in integrity.

10:2 Treasures gained by wickedness do not profit, but righteousness delivers from death.

10:9–10 Whoever walks in integrity walks securely, but he who makes his ways crooked will be found out. Whoever winks the eye causes trouble, but a babbling fool will come to ruin.

11:1 A false balance is an abomination to the Lord, but a just weight is his delight.

11:3 The integrity of the upright guides them, but the crookedness of the treacherous destroys them.

12:5 The thoughts of the righteous are just; the counsels of the wicked are deceitful.

12:13 An evil man is ensnared by the transgression of his lips, but the righteous escapes from trouble.

13:23 The fallow ground of the poor would yield much food, but it is swept away through injustice.

14:2 Whoever walks in uprightness fears the Lord, but he who is devious in his ways despises him.

15:27 Whoever is greedy for unjust gain troubles his own household, but he who hates bribes will live.

16:8   Better is a little with righteousness than great revenues with injustice.

16:11   A just balance and scales are the Lord's; all the weights in the bag are his work.

16:30   Whoever winks his eyes plans dishonest things; he who purses his lips brings evil to pass.

17:8   A bribe is like a magic stone in the eyes of the one who gives it; wherever he turns he prospers.

17:20   A man of crooked heart does not discover good, and one with a dishonest tongue falls into calamity.

17:23   The wicked accepts a bribe in secret to pervert the ways of justice.

18:17   The one who states his case first seems right, until the other comes and examines him.

18:18   The lot puts an end to quarrels and decides between powerful contenders.

19:1   Better is a poor person who walks in his integrity than one who is crooked in speech and is a fool.

20:6–7   Many a man proclaims his own steadfast love, but a faithful man who can find? The righteous who walks in his integrity – blessed are his children after him!

20:10   Unequal weights and unequal measures are both alike an abomination to the Lord.

20:14   "Bad, Bad," says the buyer, but when he goes away, then he boasts.

20:17   Bread gained by deceit is sweet to a man, but afterward his mouth will be full of gravel.

20:23   Unequal weights are an abomination to the Lord, and false scales are not good.

21:21   Whoever pursues righteousness and kindness will find life, righteousness, and honor.

22:16   Whoever oppresses the poor to increase his own wealth, or gives to the rich, will only come to poverty.

23:10–12   Do not move an ancient landmark or enter the fields of the fatherless, for their Redeemer is strong; he will plead their cause against you. Apply your heart to instruction and your ear to words of knowledge.

28:6   Better is a poor man who walks in his integrity than a rich man who is crooked in his ways.

28:16   A ruler who lacks understanding is a cruel oppressor, but he who hates unjust gain will prolong his days.

28:18   Whoever walks in integrity will be delivered, but he who is crooked in his ways will suddenly fall.

28:21   To show partiality is not good, but for a piece of bread a man will do wrong.

29:4   By justice a king builds up the land, but he who exacts gifts tears it down.

29:24   The partner of a thief hates his own life; he hears the curse, but discloses nothing.

29:26   Many seek the face of a ruler, but it is from the Lord that a man gets justice.

Surety

6:1   My son, if you have put up security for your neighbor, have given your pledge for a stranger.

11:15   Whoever puts up security for a stranger will surely suffer harm, but he who hates striking hands in pledge is secure.

17:18   One who lacks sense gives a pledge and puts up security in the presence of his neighbor.

20:16   Take a man's garment when he has put up security for a stranger, and hold it in pledge when he puts up security for foreigners.

22:26–27   Be not one of those who give pledges, who put up security for debts. If you have nothing with which to pay, why should your bed be taken from under you?

27:13   Take a man's garment when he has put up security for a stranger, and hold it in pledge when he puts up security for an adulteress.

Truth/Honesty

2:15 Men whose paths are crooked, and who are devious in their ways.

3:3 Let not steadfast love and faithfulness forsake you; bind them around your neck; write them on the tablet of your heart.

3:32 For the devious person is an abomination to the Lord, but the upright are in his confidence.

4:24 Put away from you crooked speech, and put devious talk far from you.

8:7–8 For my mouth will utter truth; wickedness is an abomination to my lips. All the words of my mouth are righteous; there is nothing twisted or crooked in them.

11:1 A false balance is an abomination to the Lord, but a just weight is his delight.

12:17 Whoever speaks the truth gives honest evidence, but a false witness utters deceit.

12:19 Truthful lips endure forever, but a lying tongue is but for a moment.

12:22 Lying lips are an abomination to the Lord, but those who act faithfully are his delight.

13:11 Wealth gained hastily will dwindle, but whoever gathers little by little will increase it.

14:2 Whoever walks in uprightness fears the Lord, but he who is devious in his ways despises him.

14:22 Do they not go astray who devise evil? Those who devise good meet steadfast love and faithfulness.

14:25 A truthful witness saves lives, but one who breathes out lies is deceitful.

16:6 By steadfast love and faithfulness iniquity is atoned for, and by the fear of the Lord one turns away from evil.

17:20 A man of crooked heart does not discover good, and one with a dishonest tongue falls into calamity.

20:28 Steadfast love and faithfulness preserve the king, and by steadfast love his throne is upheld.

21:8   The way of the guilty is crooked, but the conduct of the pure is upright.

21:28   A false witness will perish, but the word of a man who hears will endure.

22:21   To make you know what is right and true, that you may give a true answer to those who sent you?

23:23   Buy truth, and do not sell it; buy wisdom, instruction, and understanding.

28:6   Better is a poor man who walks in his integrity than a rich man who is crooked in his ways.

29:14   If a king faithfully judges the poor, his throne will be established forever.

30:7–8   Two things I ask of you; deny them not to me before I die: Remove far from me falsehood and lying; give me neither poverty nor riches; feed me with the food that is needful for me.

Wealth/Riches/Prosperity/Poverty

1:13   We shall find all precious goods, we shall fill our houses with plunder.

2:4   If you seek it like silver and search for it as for hidden treasures.

3:9   Honor the Lord with your wealth and with the firstfruits of all your produce.

3:14   For the gain from her is better than gain from silver and her profit better than gold.

3:16   Long life is in her right hand; in her left hand are riches and honor.

6:11   And poverty will come upon you like a robber, and want like an armed man.

8:10–11   Take my instruction instead of silver, and knowledge rather than choice gold, for wisdom is better than jewels, and all that you may desire cannot compare with her.

8:18–21   Riches and honor are with me, enduring wealth and righteousness. My fruit is better than gold, even fine gold, and my yield than choice silver. I walk in the way of righteousness, in the paths of justice, granting an inheritance to those who love me, and filling their treasuries.

10:4   A slack hand causes poverty, but the hand of the diligent makes rich.

10:15–16   A rich man's wealth is his strong city; the poverty of the poor is their ruin. The wage of the righteous leads to life, the gain of the wicked to sin.

10:20   The tongue of the righteous is choice silver; the heart of the wicked is of little worth.

10:22   The blessing of the Lord makes rich, and he adds no sorrow with it.

11:4   Riches do not profit in the day of wrath, but righteousness delivers from death.

11:16   A gracious woman gets honor, and violent men get riches.

11:18   The wicked earns deceptive wages, but one who sows righteousness gets a sure reward.

11:28   Whoever trusts in his riches will fall, but the righteous will flourish like a green leaf.

11:31   If the righteous is repaid on earth, how much more the wicked and the sinner!

13:7–8   One pretends to be rich, yet has nothing; another pretends to be poor, yet has great wealth. The ransom of a man's life is his wealth, but a poor man hears no threat.

13:11   Wealth gained hastily will dwindle, but whoever gathers little by little will increase it.

13:13   Whoever despises the word brings destruction on himself, but he who reveres the commandment will be rewarded.

13:18   Poverty and disgrace come to him who ignores instruction, but whoever heeds reproof is honored.

13:21–23   Disaster pursues sinners, but the righteous are rewarded with good. A good man leaves an inheritance to his children's children, but the sinner's wealth is laid up for the righteous. The fallow ground of the poor would yield much food, but it is swept away through injustice.

14:20–21 The poor is disliked even by his neighbor, but the rich has many friends. Whoever despises his neighbor is a sinner, but blessed is he who is generous to the poor.

14:23–24 In all toil there is profit, but mere talk tends only to poverty. The crown of the wise is their wealth, but the folly of fools brings folly.

14:31 Whoever oppresses a poor man insults his Maker, but he who is generous to the needy honors him.

15:6 In the house of the righteous there is much treasure, but trouble befalls the income of the wicked.

15:16 Better is a little with the fear of the Lord than great treasure and trouble with it.

16:16 How much better to get wisdom than gold! To get understanding is to be chosen rather than silver.

17:2 A servant who deals wisely will rule over a son who acts shamefully and will share the inheritance as one of the brothers.

17:5 Whoever mocks the poor insults his Maker; he who is glad at calamity will not go unpunished.

18:11 A rich man's wealth is his strong city, and like a high wall in his imagination.

18:23 The poor use entreaties, but the rich answer roughly.

19:1 Better is a poor person who walks in his integrity than one who is crooked in speech and is a fool.

19:4 Wealth brings many new friends, but a poor man is deserted by his friend.

19:6–7 Many seek the favor of a generous man, and everyone is a friend to a man who gives gifts. All a poor man's brothers hate him; how much more do his friends go far from him! He pursues them with words, but does not have them.

19:10 It is not fitting for a fool to live in luxury, much less for a slave to rule over princes.

19:14 House and wealth are inherited from fathers, but a prudent wife is from the Lord.

19:17 Whoever is generous to the poor lends to the Lord, and he will repay him for his deed.

19:22   What is desired in a man is steadfast love, and a poor man is better than a liar.

20:13   Love not sleep, lest you come to poverty; open your eyes, and you will have plenty of bread.

20:15   There is gold and abundance of costly stones, but the lips of knowledge are a precious jewel.

20:21   An inheritance gained hastily in the beginning will not be blessed in the end.

21:5–6   The plans of the diligent lead surely to abundance, but everyone who is hasty comes only to poverty. The getting of treasures by a lying tongue is a fleeting vapor and a snare of death.

21:13   Whoever closes his ear to the cry of the poor will himself call out and not be answered.

21:17   Whoever loves pleasure will be a poor man; he who loves wine and oil will not be rich.

21:20   Precious treasure and oil are in a wise man's dwelling, but a foolish man devours it.

22:1–2   A good name is to be chosen rather than great riches, and favor is better than silver or gold. The rich and the poor meet together; the Lord is the maker of them all.

22:4   The reward for humility and fear of the Lord is riches and honor and life.

22:7   The rich rules over the poor, and the borrower is the slave of the lender.

22:9   Whoever has a bountiful eye will be blessed, for he shares his bread with the poor.

22:16   Whoever oppresses the poor to increase his own wealth, or gives to the rich, will only come to poverty.

22:22   Do not rob the poor, because he is poor, or crush the afflicted at the gate.

23:4–5   Do not toil to acquire wealth; be discerning enough to desist. When your eyes light on it, it is gone, for suddenly it sprouts wings, flying like an eagle toward heaven.

23:17–21   Let not your heart envy sinners, but continue in the fear of the Lord all the day. Surely there is a future, and your hope will not be cut off. Hear, my son, and be wise, and direct your heart in the way. Be not among drunkards or among gluttonous eaters of meat, for the drunkard and the glutton will come to poverty, and slumber will clothe them with rags.

24:4   By knowledge the rooms are filled with all precious and pleasant riches.

24:34   And poverty will come upon you like a robber, and want like an armed man.

25:21–22   If your enemy is hungry, give him bread to eat, and if he is thirsty, give him water to drink, for you will heap burning coals on his head, and the Lord will reward you.

27:24   For riches do not last forever; and does a crown endure to all generations?

28:3   A poor man who oppresses the poor is a beating rain that leaves no food.

28:6   Better is a poor man who walks in his integrity than a rich man who is crooked in his ways.

28:8   Whoever multiplies his wealth by interest and profit gathers it for him who is generous to the poor.

28:11   A rich man is wise in his own eyes, but a poor man who has understanding will find him out.

28:19   Whoever works his land will have plenty of bread, but he who follows worthless pursuits will have plenty of poverty.

28:20   A faithful man will abound with blessings, but whoever hastens to be rich will not go unpunished.

28:22   A stingy man hastens after wealth and does not know that poverty will come upon him.

28:27   Whoever gives to the poor will not want, but he who hides his eyes will get many a curse.

29:3   He who loves wisdom makes his father glad, but a companion of prostitutes squanders his wealth.

29:7   A righteous man knows the rights of the poor; a wicked man does not understand such knowledge.

29:13–14   The poor man and the oppressor meet together; the Lord gives light to the eyes of both. If a king faithfully judges the poor, his throne will be established forever.

30:7–9   Two things I ask of you; deny them not to me before I die: Remove far from me falsehood and lying; give me neither poverty nor riches; feed me with the food that is needful for me, lest I be full and deny you and say, "Who is the Lord?" or lest I be poor and steal and profane the name of my God.

31:20   She opens her hand to the poor and reaches out her hands to the needy.

Work/Labor

6:6–11   Go to the ant, O sluggard; consider her ways, and be wise. Without having any chief, officer, or ruler, she prepares her bread in summer and gathers her food in harvest. How long will you lie there, O sluggard? When will you arise from your sleep? A little sleep, a little slumber, a little folding of the hands to rest, and poverty will come upon you like a robber, and want like an armed man.

10:4–5   A slack hand causes poverty, but the hand of the diligent makes rich. He who gathers in summer is a prudent son, but he who sleeps in harvest is a son who brings shame.

10:26   Like vinegar to the teeth and smoke to the eyes, so is the sluggard to those who send him.

12:11   Whoever works his land will have plenty of bread, but he who follows worthless pursuits lacks sense.

12:14   From the fruit of his mouth a man is satisfied with good, and the work of a man's hand comes back to him.

12:24   The hand of the diligent will rule, while the slothful will be put to forced labor.

12:27   Whoever is slothful will not roast his game, but the diligent man will get precious wealth.

13:4   The soul of the sluggard craves and gets nothing, while the soul of the diligent is richly supplied.

13:11   Wealth gained hastily will dwindle, but whoever gathers little by little will increase it.

13:23   The fallow ground of the poor would yield much food, but it is swept away through injustice.

14:4   Where there are no oxen, the manger is clean, but abundant crops come by the strength of the ox.

14:23   In all toil there is profit, but mere talk tends only to poverty.

15:19   The way of a sluggard is like a hedge of thorns, but the path of the upright is a level highway.

16:3   Commit your work to the Lord, and your plans will be established.

16:26   A worker's appetite works for him; his mouth urges him on.

18:9   Whoever is slack in his work is a brother to him who destroys.

19:15   Slothfulness casts into a deep sleep, and an idle person will suffer hunger.

19:24   The sluggard buries his hand in the dish and will not even bring it back to his mouth.

20:4   The sluggard does not plow in the autumn; he will seek at harvest and have nothing.

20:13   Love not sleep, lest you come to poverty; open your eyes, and you will have plenty of bread.

21:5   The plans of the diligent lead surely to abundance, but everyone who is hasty comes only to poverty.

21:17   Whoever loves pleasure will be a poor man; he who loves wine and oil will not be rich.

21:25–26   The desire of the sluggard kills him, for his hands refuse to labor. All day long he craves and craves, but the righteous gives and does not hold back.

22:13   The sluggard says, "There is a lion outside! I shall be killed in the streets!"

22:29   Do you see a man skillful in his work? He will stand before kings; he will not stand before obscure men.

24:10–12 If you faint in the day of adversity, your strength is small. Rescue those who are being taken away to death; hold back those who are stumbling to the slaughter. If you say, "Behold, we did not know this," does not he who weighs the heart perceive it? Does not he who keeps watch over your soul know it, and will he not repay man according to his work?

24:27 Prepare your work outside; get everything ready for yourself in the field, and after that build your house.

24:29 Do not say, "I will do to him as he has done to me; I will pay the man back for what he has done."

24:30–34 I passed by the field of a sluggard, by the vineyard of a man lacking sense, and behold, it was all overgrown with thorns; the ground was covered with nettles, and its stone wall was broken down. Then I saw and considered it; I looked and received instruction. A little sleep, a little slumber, a little folding of the hands to rest, and poverty will come upon you like a robber, and want like an armed man.

26:13–16 The sluggard says, "There is a lion in the road! There is a lion in the streets!" As a door turns on its hinges, so does a sluggard on his bed. The sluggard buries his hand in the dish; it wears him out to bring it back to his mouth. The sluggard is wiser in his own eyes than seven men who can answer sensibly.

27:23–27 Know well the condition of your flocks, and give attention to your herds, for riches do not last forever; and does a crown endure to all generations? When the grass is gone and the new growth appears and the vegetation of the mountains is gathered, the lambs will provide your clothing, and the goats the price of a field. There will be enough goats' milk for your food, for the food of your household and maintenance for your girls.

28:19 Whoever works his land will have plenty of bread, but he who follows worthless pursuits will have plenty of poverty.

31:13 She seeks wool and flax, and works with willing hands.

31:31 Give her of the fruit of her hands, and let her works praise her in the gates.

11

SOCIETAL WISDOM

Benevolence/Grace/Mercy

3:3   Let not steadfast love and faithfulness forsake you; bind them around your neck; write them on the tablet of your heart.

3:27–30   Do not withhold good from those to whom it is due, when it is in your power to do it. Do not say to your neighbor, "Go, and come again, tomorrow I will give it" – when you have it with you. Do not plan evil against your neighbor, who dwells trustingly beside you. Do not contend with a man for no reason, when he has done you no harm.

4:9   She will place on your head a graceful garland; she will bestow on you a beautiful crown.

11:16–17   A gracious woman gets honor, and violent men get riches. A man who is kind benefits himself, but a cruel man hurts himself.

11:24–26   One gives freely, yet grows all the richer; another withholds what he should give, and only suffers want. Whoever brings blessing will be enriched, and one who waters will himself be watered. The people curse him who holds back grain, but a blessing is on the head of him who sells it.

14:21   Whoever despises his neighbor is a sinner, but blessed is he who is generous to the poor.

14:22   Do they not go astray who devise evil? Those who devise good meet steadfast love and faithfulness.

14:31   Whoever oppresses a poor man insults his Maker, but he who is generous to the needy honors him.

15:25   The Lord tears down the house of the proud but maintains the widow's boundaries.

17:5   Whoever mocks the poor insults his Maker; he who is glad at calamity will not go unpunished.

17:9   Whoever covers an offense seeks love, but he who repeats a matter separates close friends.

18:16   A man's gift makes room for him and brings him before the great.

19:6   Many seek the favor of a generous man, and everyone is a friend to a man who gives gifts.

19:11   Good sense makes one slow to anger, and it is his glory to overlook an offense.

19:17   Whoever is generous to the poor lends to the Lord, and he will repay him for his deed.

19:22   What is desired in a man is steadfast love, and a poor man is better than a liar.

21:13   Whoever closes his ear to the cry of the poor will himself call out and not be answered.

21:26   All day long he craves and craves, but the righteous gives and does not hold back.

22:2   The rich and the poor meet together; the Lord is the maker of them all.

22:9   Whoever has a bountiful eye will be blessed, for he shares his bread with the poor.

22:11   He who loves purity of heart, and whose speech is gracious, will have the king as his friend.

22:16   Whoever oppresses the poor to increase his own wealth, or gives to the rich, will only come to poverty.

22:22–23   Do not rob the poor, because he is poor, or crush the afflicted at the gate, for the Lord will plead their cause and rob of life those who rob them.

23:10–11   Do not move an ancient landmark or enter the fields of the fatherless, for their Redeemer is strong; he will plead their cause against you.

24:17–18   Do not rejoice when your enemy falls, and let not your heart be glad when he stumbles, lest the Lord see it and be displeased, and turn away his anger from him.

24:28–29   Be not a witness against your neighbor without cause, and do not deceive with your lips. Do not say, "I will do to him as he has done to me; I will pay the man back for what he has done."

25:21–22   If your enemy is hungry, give him bread to eat, and if he is thirsty, give him water to drink, for you will heap burning coals on his head, and the Lord will reward you.

28:3   A poor man who oppresses the poor is a beating rain that leaves no food.

28:8   Whoever multiplies his wealth by interest and profit gathers it for him who is generous to the poor.

28:22   A stingy man hastens after wealth and does not know that poverty will come upon him.

28:27   Whoever gives to the poor will not want, but he who hides his eyes will get many a curse.

29:7   A righteous man knows the rights of the poor; a wicked man does not understand such knowledge.

29:13   The poor man and the oppressor meet together; the Lord gives light to the eyes of both.

29:14   If a king faithfully judges the poor, his throne will be established forever.

31:20   She opens her hand to the poor and reaches out her hands to the needy.

31:26   She opens her mouth with wisdom, and the teaching of kindness is on her tongue.

Friendship/Neighbor

3:27–29   Do not withhold good from those to whom it is due, when it is in your power to do it. Do not say to your neighbor, "Go, and come again, tomorrow I will give it" – when you have it with you. Do not plan evil against your neighbor, who dwells trustingly beside you.

6:1–5   My son, if you have put up security for your neighbor, have given your pledge for a stranger, if you are snared in the words of your mouth, caught in the words of your mouth, then do this, my son, and save yourself, for you have come into the hand of your neighbor: go, hasten, and plead urgently with your neighbor. Give your eyes no sleep and your eyelids no slumber; save yourself like a gazelle from the hand of the hunter, like a bird from the hand of the fowler.

6:27–29   Can a man carry fire next to his chest and his clothes not be burned? Or can one walk on hot coals and his feet not be scorched? So is he who goes in to his neighbor's wife; none who touches her will go unpunished.

11:9   With his mouth the godless man would destroy his neighbor, but by knowledge the righteous are delivered.

11:12   Whoever belittles his neighbor lacks sense, but a man of understanding remains silent.

12:26   One who is righteous is a guide to his neighbor, but the way of the wicked leads them astray.

13:20   Whoever walks with the wise becomes wise, but the companion of fools will suffer harm.

14:20   The poor is disliked even by his neighbor, but the rich has many friends.

14:21   Whoever despises his neighbor is a sinner, but blessed is he who is generous to the poor.

16:29   A man of violence entices his neighbor and leads him in a way that is not good.

17:17   A friend loves at all times, and a brother is born for adversity.

18:19   A brother offended is more unyielding than a strong city, and quarreling is like the bars of a castle.

18:24   A man of many companions may come to ruin, but there is a friend who sticks closer than a brother.

19:4   Wealth brings many new friends, but a poor man is deserted by his friend.

19:6–7   Many seek the favor of a generous man, and everyone is a friend to a man who gives gifts. All a poor man's brothers hate him; how much more do his friends go far from him! He pursues them with words, but does not have them.

21:10   The soul of the wicked desires evil; his neighbor finds no mercy in his eyes.

22:11   He who loves purity of heart, and whose speech is gracious, will have the king as his friend.

22:24–25   Make no friendship with a man given to anger, nor go with a wrathful man, lest you learn his ways and entangle yourself in a snare.

24:21–22   My son, fear the Lord and the king, and do not join with those who do otherwise, for disaster from them will rise suddenly, and who knows the ruin that will come from them both?

24:28–29   Be not a witness against your neighbor without cause, and do not deceive with your lips. Do not say, "I will do to him as he has done to me; I will pay the man back for what he has done."

25:8–10   Do not hastily bring into court, for what will you do in the end, when your neighbor puts you to shame? Argue your case with your neighbor himself, and do not reveal another's secret, lest he who hears you bring shame upon you, and your ill repute have no end.

25:17   Let your foot be seldom in your neighbor's house, lest he have his fill of you and hate you.

25:18   A man who bears false witness against his neighbor is like a war club, or a sword, or a sharp arrow.

26:18–19   Like a madman who throws firebrands, arrows, and death is the man who deceives his neighbor and says, "I am only joking!"

27:6   Faithful are the wounds of a friend; profuse are the kisses of an enemy.

27:9–10   Oil and perfume make the heart glad, and the sweetness of a friend comes from his earnest counsel. Do not forsake your friend and your father's friend, and do not go to your brother's house in the day of your calamity. Better is a neighbor who is near than a brother who is far away.

27:14   Whoever blesses his neighbor with a loud voice, rising early in the morning, will be counted as cursing.

27:17   Iron sharpens iron, and one man sharpens another.

28:7   The one who keeps the law is a son with understanding, but a companion of gluttons shames his father.

28:24   Whoever robs his father or his mother and says, "That is no transgression," is a companion to a man who destroys.

29:3   He who loves wisdom makes his father glad, but a companion of prostitutes squanders his wealth.

29:5   A man who flatters his neighbor spreads a net for his feet.

Government/Kings

8:15–16   By me kings reign, and rulers decree what is just; by me princes rule, and nobles, all who govern justly.

11:10   When it goes well with the righteous, the city rejoices, and when the wicked perish there are shouts of gladness.

12:24   The hand of the diligent will rule, while the slothful will be put to forced labor.

14:28   In a multitude of people is the glory of a king, but without people a prince is ruined.

14:35   A servant who deals wisely has the king's favor, but his wrath falls on one who acts shamefully.

16:10   An oracle is on the lips of a king; his mouth does not sin in judgment.

16:12–15   It is an abomination to kings to do evil, for the throne is established by righteousness. Righteous lips are the delight of a king, and he loves him who speaks what is right. A king's wrath is a messenger of death, and a wise man will appease it. In the light of a the Lord; he turns it wherever he will.

22:7   The rich rules over the poor, and the borrower is the slave of the lender.

22:11   He who loves purity of heart, and whose speech is gracious, will have the king as his friend.

22:29   Do you see a man skillful in his work? He will stand before kings; he will not stand before obscure men.

23:1–3   When you sit down to eat with a ruler, observe carefully what is before you, and put a knife to your throat if you are given to appetite. Do not desire his delicacies, for they are deceptive food.

24:21–22   My son, fear the Lord and the king, and do not join with those who do otherwise, for disaster from them will rise suddenly, and who knows the ruin that will come from them both?

25:1–7   These also are proverbs of Solomon which the men of Hezekiah king of Judah copied. It is the glory of God to conceal things, but the glory of kings is to search things out. As the heavens for height, and the earth for depth, so the heart of kings is unsearchable. Take away the dross from the silver, and the smith has material for a vessel; take away the wicked from the presence of the king, and his throne will be established in righteousness. Do not put yourself forward in the king's presence or stand in the place of the great, for it is better to be told, "Come up here," than to be put lower in the presence of a noble.

25:15   With patience a ruler may be persuaded, and a soft tongue will break a bone.

28:2   When a land transgresses, it has many rulers, but with a man of understanding and knowledge, its stability will long continue.

28:15   Like a roaring lion or a charging bear is a wicked ruler over a poor people.

28:16   A ruler who lacks understanding is a cruel oppressor, but he who hates unjust gain will prolong his days.

29:2   When the righteous increase, the people rejoice, but when the wicked rule, the people groan.

29:4   By justice a king builds up the land, but he who exacts gifts tears it down.

29:12   If a ruler listens to falsehood, all his officials will be wicked.

29:14   If a king faithfully judges the poor, his throne will be established forever.

29:26   Many seek the face of a ruler, but it is from the Lord that a man gets justice.

30:21–23   Under three things the earth trembles; under four it cannot bear up: a slave when he becomes king, and a fool when he is filled with food; an unloved woman when she gets a husband, and a maidservant when she displaces her mistress.

30:29–31   Three things are stately in their tread; four are stately in their stride: the lion, which is mightiest among beasts and does not turn back before any; the strutting rooster, the he–goat, and a king whose army is with him.

31:3–4   Do not give your strength to women, your ways to those who destroy kings. It is not for kings, O Lemuel, it is not for kings to drink wine, or for rulers to take strong drink.

Name/Reputation

3:3–4   Let not steadfast love and faithfulness forsake you; bind them around your neck; write them on the tablet of your heart. So you will find favor and good success in the sight of God and man.

10:7   The memory of the righteous is a blessing, but the name of the wicked will rot.

22:1   A good name is to be chosen rather than great riches, and favor is better than silver or gold.

31:31   Give her of the fruit of her hands, and let her works praise her in the gates.

APPENDIX ONE –
OLD TESTAMENT PROVERBS
IN THE NEW TESTAMENT

1:16	Romans 3:15	20:27	1 Corinthians 2:11
2:3-6	James 1:5	22:9	2 Corinthians 9:6
2:4	Matthew 13:44	23:4	1 Timothy 6:9
3:3	2 Corinthians 3:3	24:12	Matthew 16:27;
3:4	Luke 2:52		Luke 16:15; Romans 2:6;
3:7	Romans 12:16		2 Timothy 4:14; 1 Peter
3:11-12	Hebrews 12:5-6		1:17; Revelation 2:23;
3:34	James 4:6; 1 Peter 5:5		20:12-13; 22:12
7:3	2 Corinthians 3:3	24:21	1 Peter 2:17
8:15-16	Romans 13:1	25:6-7	Luke 14:8-10
10:12	James 5:20; 1 Peter 4:8	25:21-22	Romans 12:20
11:24-25	2 Corinthians 9:6	26:11	2 Peter 2:22
11:31	1 Peter 4:18	27:1	James 4:13-14
17:3	1 Peter 1:7	28:13	1 John 1:9
19:17	Matthew 25:40	29:23	Matthew 23:12
19:18	Ephesians 6:4	30:4	John 3:13
20:22	1 Thessalonians 5:15		

DEVOTIONAL INDEX

1. Spiritual Wisdom

2. Personal Wisdom

LIFE-APPLICATION INDEX

PROVERBS INDEX

6:1–3 166, 176
6:1–5 214
6:2 154
6:3 37
6:6 144, 183
6:6–8 42, 76
6:6–11 208
6:11 203
6:12 108, 138, 154
6:12–15 83
6:14 116, 130
6:15 127
6:16 136
6:16–17 148
6:16–19 79, 89
6:17 116, 138, 154
6:18 108, 130, 144
6:19 116, 138, 154
6:20 37, 164
6:20–23 166, 176
6:21 130
6:22 119, 154
6:23 96, 144, 169, 171
6:24 154, 164
6:24–35 141–142
6:25 130
6:27–29 214
6:29 173
6:34 116

Proverbs 7
7:1 37, 154
7:1–2 164
7:1–5 166–167, 176
7:3 130
7:4 183, 191
7:5 154, 164
7:5–27 142
7:10 130
7:18 136
7:21 154
7:22 121
7:23 96, 194

7:24 154
7:25 130, 144
7:27 96

Proverbs 8
8:1 191
8:1–36 183–184
8:1–36 51
8:5 121
8:6 101
8:6–8 154
8:7 79, 108
8:7–8 202
8:8 101
8:9 101, 191
8:9–10 194
8:10–11 203
8:11 69, 150
8:12 195
8:13 32, 83, 86, 89, 136, 145, 148, 154
8:14 119, 191
8:15 101
8:15–16 216
8:17 136
8:18 101, 134
8:18–21 203–204
8:19 69, 150
8:20 145
8:20–21 101
8:21 136
8:22–31 41, 82, 89
8:30 87
8:32 80, 145, 154, 164
8:34 81
8:35 89
8:35–36 81, 96
8:36 108, 136

Proverbs 9
9:1–12 184–185
9:4 191
9:6 121, 145, 164, 191

SUBJECT INDEX

THEMATIC INDEX

STRATEGY FOR SPIRITUAL SUCCESS WORKSHEET

WEEK:_____ LIFE APPLICATON:_____
THEME(S):_____

1. What godly life activities/styles are wisely promoted?

2. What sinful life activities/styles are wisely prohibited?

3. How will the foolishness of potential sin in my life be prevented?

4. How will the foolishness of actual sin in my life be remedied?

5. What will I specifically change in order to live more wisely?

Permission is granted to freely reproduce this sample worksheet

Christian Focus Publications

We publishes books for all ages. Our mission statement:

STAYING FAITHFUL

In dependence upon God, we seek to help make his infallible word, the Bible, relevant. Our aim is to ensure that the Lord Jesus Christ is presented as the only hope to obtain forgiveness of sin, live a useful life, and look forward to heaven with him.

REACHING OUT

Christ's last command requires us to reach out to our world with his gospel. We seek to help fulfill that by publishing books that point people towards Jesus and for them to develop a Christ-like maturity. We aim to equip all levels of readers for life, work, ministry and mission.

Books in our adult range are published in three imprints.

Christian Heritage contains classic writings from the past.
Mentor focuses on books written at a level suitable for Bible College and seminary students, pastors, and other serious readers; the imprint includes commentaries, doctrinal studies, examination of current issues, and church history.
Christian Focus contains popular works including biographies, commentaries, basic doctrine, and Christian living. Our children's books are also published in this imprint.

For a free catalogue of all our titles, please write to:
Christian Focus Publications, Ltd
Geanies House, Fearn,
Ross-shire, IV20 1TW, Scotland,
United Kingdom
info@christianfocus.com

For details of our titles, visit us on our website
www.christianfocus.com

Tengo un gato

1ª Parte, Unidad 8

Barbara Scanes and Jenny Bell

2

3

Vocabulario

me gusta	I like
ya	already
no me gusta	I don't like
un poni	a pony
un gato	a cat
el gato	the cat
mi gato	my cat
tu gato	your cat
un perro	a dog
los perros	(the) dogs
odio	I hate
(él) odia	he hates
(ella) odia	she hates
un conejo	a rabbit
el gato se come	the cat eats
una serpiente	a snake
una rata	a rat
un animal	a (pet) animal
un pez	a fish
un hámster	a hamster
dos hámsteres	two hamsters
me encanta	I love